52 Weekly Habits

Enhance Your Health and Happiness
with Small Actions

Paula Castellon
Vancouver, BC

For my children, except my oldest, who's had enough of self-help books in this lifetime.

1. Introduction — 7
- What are Habits? — 8
- Simplified Personality Tendency Test — 9
- Understanding Your Tendency — 10
- Why Forming Habits is so Challenging — 12
- Habit Stacking — 13
- Tips for Success — 13

2. Instructions for the Workbook — 15
- Know Your 'Why' — 19

3. Let's Begin — 21
- Week 1: Practice Deep Breathing — 21
- Week 2: Drink More Water — 24
- Week 3: 2min Stretch — 26
- Week 4: Practice Good Posture — 28
- Week 5: Journaling — 30
- Week 6: Mindful Eating — 32
- Week 7: Daily Walking — 34
- Week 8: Improve Sleep Routine — 36
- Week 9: Decluttering — 38
- Week 10: Reduce Screen Time — 40
- Week 11: Healthy Snacking — 42
- Week 12: Oil Pulling — 44
- Week 13: Morning Meditation — 46
- Week 14: Morning Affirmations — 48
- Week 15: Morning Phone Detox — 50
- Week 16: Night Time Phone Detox — 52
- Week 17: Practice Kindness — 54
- Week 18: Read Before Bed — 56
- Week 19: Do something Uncomfortable — 58
- Week 20: Early Morning Rise — 60
- Week 21: Sugar Free Day — 62
- Week 22: Have a Buddha Smile — 64
- Week 23: Conscious Breathing — 66
- Week 24: Morning Sun Salutation — 68

Week 25: Take the Stairs	72
Week 26: Mid-Year Reflection	**74**
Week 27: Create a Vision Board	78
Week 28: Nighttime Routine	80
Week 29: Fast After Dinner	82
Week 30: Explore Nature	84
Week 31: Learn Something New	86
Week 32: Write a Letter	88
Week 33: Express Gratitude	90
Week 34: Squats while you Brush	92
Week 35: Reconnect with Someone You Lost Touch With	94
Week 36: Make your bed	96
Week 37: Listen to a Podcast	98
Week 38: No Complaints Day	100
Week 39: Explore a New Place	102
Week 40: Focus on Your Work	104
Week 41:Learn to Say No	106
Week 42:Learn to Say Yes	108
Week 43: Correct Something you Are Doing Wrong	110
Week 44: Daily Laughter	112
Week 45: Avoid Processed Food	114
Week 46: Learn a New Word	116
Week 47: Early Dinner	118
Week 48: Practice Patience	120
Week 49: Practice Forgiveness	122
Week 50: Allow Something to Take your Breath Away	126
Week 51: Reflect on Achievements	128
Week 52: Plan for the Next Year	130
4. You are Fabulous	**133**
5. Appendix	**134**

1. Introduction

Welcome to "52 Weekly Habits," a journey that brings motivation, awareness, and transformative change into your life by focusing on the small things. Each week, you'll be guided through simple habits[1] that lead to improved health, well-being, personal growth, and the satisfaction of knowing you are continually working towards your fullest potential. Significant change often starts with small, manageable steps. We are living longer than ever before, so invest in a healthy and fulfilling life forward.

If you're anything like me, sticking to new health habits is a bit of a stretch. Maybe it feels overwhelming, the goals are too ambitious or unsustainable, you require accountability from another person, or the purpose behind the effort isn't clear to you. Or, hey, maybe it's just tough to get into new routines. In this workbook we're going to take on 52 small, doable changes that make your life a little better – nothing too scary, I promise. We'll tackle one tiny habit a week, and we'll do it together. I encourage you to join our supportive community at www.52WeeklyHabits.com. Your entire life can really change in a year, because the accumulation of small, consistent actions is what leads to substantial and lasting changes over time.

This workbook is designed as an approachable and engaging way to help people who struggle with consistency or self-motivation (which is almost everyone) to slowly integrate healthier routines into their lives. By breaking down the process into manageable weekly tasks, it makes the journey less overwhelming and more achievable.

In this process you'll embark on a journey of self-improvement, designed to introduce you to the transformative power of habit stacking—a method that involves adding small, manageable habits into your daily routine, one week at a time. More on this to follow.

But there's more. We've designed this journey to fit your unique personality when it comes to being accountable, borrowing from Gretchen Rubin's insightful 'Four Tendencies' framework. This personality model, developed from Rubin's analysis of over 600,000 responses to her online questionnaire, categorizes people based on how they respond to internal and external

---

[1] Typically a habit is an action we perform automatically, often without thinking about it. This book offers actions that will hopefully turn to habits.

expectations. By understanding which of the four unique tendencies you align with, you'll gain insight into your motivational drivers. This framework is instrumental in guiding you through the next 52 weeks, to form lasting habits or make life changes in a way that resonates with your individual nature. Following, will be a quick personality tendency test based on Rubin's framework so that you can better understand your challenges and how you are best motivated.

What are Habits?

"Habits" are routines of behaviors that are repeated regularly and tend to occur subconsciously. They are actions or patterns of behavior that have become automatic through frequent repetition. Habits can be both positive and negative, and they play a significant role in daily life, influencing a person's way of living, working, and interacting with others.

How long does it take to turn a behavior into a habit, so it becomes as automatic as brushing your teeth?

The time needed to turn a new behavior into a habit can vary significantly, depending on the complexity of the behavior, the individual (ie your personality tendency) and the circumstances. A commonly cited figure is 21 days, which originated from Dr. Maxwell Maltz's observations in the 1960s. However, a study cited by Phillippa Lally and her team at University College London found that, on average, it takes about 66 days for a new behavior to become automatic or habitual. The study also noted that this can vary: it can take anywhere from 18 to 254 days. The key takeaway is that habit formation is a gradual process and requires consistent repetition over time.

> "
> Success is the sum of small efforts, repeated day in and day out.
> Robert Collier
> "

Simplified Personality Tendency Test[1]

Instructions: For each question select the answer that best resonates with you.

1. When setting personal goals, do you:

- A) Stick to them easily
- B) Need external deadlines
- C) Struggle unless someone else is counting on you
- D) Resist setting them

2. How do you respond to a work deadline?

- A) I meet it comfortably
- B) I question its necessity
- C) I meet it because others rely on me
- D) I dislike being told what to do

3. In your personal life, are you more likely to:

- A) Follow a routine
- B) Create an outline only if it makes sense to you
- C) Need reminders from others
- D) Resist routines

4. When given a task, do you:

- A) Complete it without question
- B) Analyze its importance first
- C) Do it if someone else is depending on yo
- D) Want to do it your way

5. How do you react to rules?

- A) I follow them
- B) I follow them if I agree with them
- C) I follow them if others do
- D) I often break them

> " The better you understand yourself, your values, and your desires, the more effective you can be in making positive changes in your life and habits.
> — Gretchen Rubin "

Understanding Your Tendency

Now let's find out how you can best succeed and understand yourself when it comes to adopting and sticking to new habits. The revised and simplified test you completed is based on the Four Tendencies framework by Gretchen Rubin. It classifies individuals into four categories, based on how they respond to internal and external expectations. Depending if your responses where mostly a,b,c or d you can review your possible tendency below and how to best succeed in forming new habits as we move along 52 Weekly Habits:

1. **Upholder: Mostly a's**
   19% of us fall into this category
   Naturally self-disciplined (lucky!). Upholders find it easy to cultivate new habits, whether self-imposed or suggested by others. They are comfortable with structure and consistency, making them adept at maintaining routines and schedules.
   Success in Habits: Typically high, due to their self-discipline and comfort with routines.
   Recommendations: Maintain balance to avoid rigidity; prioritize self-care along with obligations to self and others.

2. **Questioner: Mostly b's**
   24% of people fall into this category
   They require logical reasons to adopt a new habit. Questioners will engage in a habit only if it makes sense to them after a thorough investigation and analysis. They value efficiency and purpose, preferring habits that are evidently beneficial.
   Success in Habits: Depends on the personal rationale behind the habit.
   Recommendations: Research or focus on understanding the purpose and efficiency of habits; create a system of self-accountability.

---

[2]For more accuracy visit gretchenrubin.com

3. **Obliger: Mostly c's**
   41% of people fall into this category
   Motivated by external accountability, Obligers often struggle to maintain habits on their own. They excel when there is external reinforcement or expectations, such as a coach, a support group, or public commitments. This external pressure is crucial for Obligers to sustain new habits.
   Success in Habits: Often struggles without external accountability.
   Recommendations: Seek external support systems, like accountability partners or groups; set up external reminders and rewards. Participate in our online community.

4. **Mostly d's: Rebel**
   17% of people fall into this category
   Valuing freedom and self-expression, Rebels resist both internal and external expectations. They adopt habits that align with their identity and give them a sense of autonomy. Rebels are more likely to engage in habits that feel like a choice or an expression of self, rather than a requirement or imposition.
   Success in Habits: Varies; often successful when habits align with their sense of identity.
   Recommendations: Choose habits that feel like an expression of freedom and self-identity; avoid feeling constrained by routines.

By understanding your tendency, as we move through the habits you'll be able to adopt strategies more aligned with your innate response to expectations, hopefully increasing your chances of successfully forming new habits. And be gentle and understanding with yourself, now that you have some insight of your personality tendency.

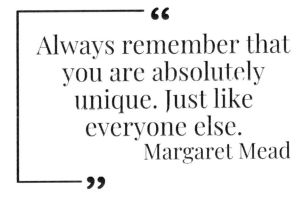

> "Always remember that you are absolutely unique. Just like everyone else."
> — Margaret Mead

Why Forming Habits is so Challenging

Maintaining habits can be challenging, and there are several reasons, backed by research and psychological theories, why we struggle so much to keep them. Here are four reasons supported by research:

1. Lack of Intrinsic Motivation: Research has shown that habits are more likely to be maintained when they are driven by intrinsic motivation. This means you are doing something because it is inherently rewarding, compared to extrinsic rewards. When motivation is external, such as for monetary rewards or external approval, it might not be as sustainable.
   Ryan, R. M., & Deci, E. L. (2000). Intrinsic and extrinsic motivations: Classic definitions and new directions. Contemporary Educational Psychology.

2. Lack of Consistency: Consistency is key in habit formation. A study in the European Journal of Social Psychology found that missing a single day did not reduce the chance of forming a habit, but inconsistency in the long term did.
   Lally, P., Van Jaarsveld, C. H. M., Potts, H. W. W., & Wardle, J. (2010). How are habits formed: Modeling habit formation in the real world.

3. Inadequate Self-Control and Willpower: Research suggests that self-control is like a muscle that can be depleted, known as "ego depletion." When we use a lot of self-control for one task, it can be harder to exert self-control for subsequent tasks, affecting habit maintenance.
   Baumeister, R.F., Vohs, K. D., & Tice, D. M. (2007). The strength model of self-control.

4. Failure to Address Underlying Behaviors: Habits are often a response to deeper psychological needs or states. Without addressing the underlying behaviors or triggers, such as stress or anxiety, it can be difficult to maintain new, healthier habits.
   Reference: Wood, W., & Neal, D. T. (2007). A new look at habits and the habit-goal interface. Psychological Review.

Understanding why you may feel challenges through this journey can help guide your strategies in ways that are more effective in habit formation and maintenance. This involves fostering internal motivation (do it for you), creating consistent routines, managing willpower, and addressing underlying psychological factors.

Habit Stacking

A technique we'll be using to help you adopt as many habits as possible is called "habit" stacking, popularized by James Clear in his book "Atomic Habits." It refers to the practice of building new habits by "stacking" them onto existing ones. The basic idea is to take a habit you already do regularly and add a new behavior to it. This technique leverages the existing routine as a cue for the new habit, making it easier to remember and establish.

For example, if you have a well-established habit of brushing your teeth every morning (existing habit), and you want to develop the habit of mindfulness (new habit), you could "stack" the new habit onto the existing one by practicing mindfulness during or right after you brush your teeth.

Habit stacking works well because it integrates the new habit into your existing routine, reducing the mental effort and willpower needed to remember to do it. By associating the new habit with an established routine, you create a linked sequence of behaviors, making the new habit feel more natural and easier to adopt.

Tips for Success

Persistence and patience will be crucial in developing new habits. For the best chance of success, be part of our online community and stay mindful of your personality tendency. With that in mind, try repeating the desired behavior in a consistent setting and find existing habits to help remind you of your new habits so that it becomes more automatic over time. It's important to note that missing a day or two does not significantly impact the habit formation process, just come back to it before too much time has passed.

Another powerful strategy is the "5 Second Rule", a simple yet powerful tool for self-motivation and action, developed by Mel Robbins. The rule is straightforward: when you have an instinct to act on a goal or a commitment, you must physically move within five seconds to act on it. The moment you have an impulse to do something that aligns with your goals or responsibilities, you count down from five to one and then physically move to take action, without overthinking it.

This rule is designed to override the brain's tendency to resist change or avoid discomfort, a process that often leads to procrastination or inaction. By reacting within that five-second window, you bypass the mental barriers and excuses that can hold you back. It's essentially a "starting ritual" that triggers activity and helps break the cycle of overthinking, hesitation, and fear. Mel Robbins explains that this rule empowers you to take control of your actions, build better habits, and live a more proactive and fulfilling life.

Here are 7 more generic tips to help you succeed, which you can use as part of your practice:

1. **Set Clear, Achievable Goals:** Define what you want to achieve with your new habit in clear, specific terms. For example, instead of a vague goal like "improve flexibility," aim for something more concrete, such as "stretch for 10 minutes every morning."

2. **Start Small and Build Gradually:** Begin with small, manageable steps. Instead of 8 waters a day, start with just one in the morning. Small successes build momentum and confidence.

3. **Establish Triggers:** Use existing routines or specific cues as triggers for your new habit. If you want to start a morning meditation practice, do it right after brushing your teeth. This links the new habit with an established action.

4. **Stay Consistent:** Consistency is crucial in habit formation. Try to perform your new habit at the same time and in the same place every day to reinforce the routine. Or set timers if you prefer less rigidity.

5. **Track Your Progress:** Keeping a record of your habits, either in this journal, on a calendar, or through an app, can be highly motivating and helps you stay accountable.

6. **Reward Yourself:** Set up a system of rewards for sticking to your habit. Rewards reinforce positive behavior and make the habit-forming process more enjoyable.

7. **Be Patient and Kind to Yourself:** Habit formation takes time, and it's normal to encounter setbacks. Keep your personality tendency in mind, be patient and understand that progress is often non-linear. If you miss a day, don't worry about it — just pick up where you left off.

2. Instructions for the Workbook

'*52 Weekly Habits*' is a workbook dedicated to creating small, achievable habits that can significantly boost your health and happiness with small changes. Each week, you'll adopt a simple new habit into your routine. These habits are super easy to fit into your busy life, especially if you normally find it tough to stick to new health habits. It encourages you to persist, reassuming your new habits whenever possible, without pressure.

Each new habit is crafted for simplicity, typically requiring no more than 10 minutes a day. You might even find many are already part of your daily life. Some you may adopt for a lifetime while others you might try just for the week. It's up to you to find the habits that work best for you, stack and tweak as needed. This workbook is more than a habit tracker; it's a tool for anyone seeking a positive shift in their health and lifestyle.

Each week we focus on a small, easy-to-implement habit. Some examples could be:

- Drink an extra glass of water each day.
- Take a ten-minute walk.
- Spend ten-minutes unplugged from electronic devices.

And so on, gradually stacking more habits as the weeks progress. I will show examples of how weekly habits can stack on each other from other weeks throughout the journal and tips to make adoption straight forward. The key is to keep these habits simple and low-effort, especially in the beginning, to encourage consistency and prevent burnout. There is also a weekly tracking sheet that I encourage you to use. In the appendix you'll find a table where you can track all the days you kept a habit, a list of all the habits so you can reference it and other helpful worksheets.

You could also incorporate elements like weekly reflections, small rewards for consistency, and tips or participate in our online community to make each habit more enjoyable or easier to stick to. This can help maintain motivation and provide a sense of accomplishment as the weeks progress.

Here are some suggestions for using this habit workbook to have your best chance of success:

1. **Start Fresh Each Monday:** Every week introduces a new habit, you can start on any week but chronological is probably the best since habits are organized in a specific order starting with simpler habits that can build on others. Starting on Monday gives you a clear beginning and a whole week to integrate this new practice into your life. If you miss a day or don't make it through the week that's okay, because any days you did are still better than none!

2. **Flexibility Is Key:** Feel free to adapt the habits to fit your schedule and preferences. Some habits might resonate more with you; feel free to focus on these more.

3. **Combine Habits for Greater Impact:** Many of these habits naturally complement each other. For example, you can practice mindful breathing during your yoga session, or reflect on your gratitude while taking a nature walk. This will become more apparent as the weeks pass and you practice new habits.

4. **Daily, Weekly, or Annual:** While each habit is introduced weekly, you can choose to practice it daily, stick to it weekly, or even adopt it as a monthly or annual practice. The frequency is up to you and what fits best in your life.

5. **Tracking and Reflection:** Use the habit tracker table to mark your progress and the reflection space to jot down your thoughts, experiences, and feelings. This will help you understand which habits are making a positive impact on your life. The last 21 days of habits will be on the table, as well as blank line for your personal input.

6. **Sticky Notes:** Write down your new habit and goal and stick it on your bathroom wall, bedside or wherever it makes sense as a daily reminder. You can remove and add as many as you want to help keep you on track.

Do your best to track your progress with the worksheets for each habit and in the appendix. They provide a structured and visually clear method to monitor progress and maintain consistency in habit development which will be especially helpful for some you. By visually marking off completed habits, it not only reinforces accountability and commitment but also enables easy assessment and adaptation of habits over time.

Know Your 'Why'

Understanding the deeper purpose behind your habit, or your *why*, can be a powerful motivator, especially for certain personality tendencies. To keep things moving and make things easier for you, each habit outlines examples of deeper purpose or a personal value driver which you can adopt as your *why* if you find it helpful. Examples include improving overall well-being, achieving personal growth, or aligning with long-term life goals. Knowing *"your why"* can provide the extra push needed to maintain your commitment, especially during challenging times.

As you turn each page, you'll find yourself building a collection of positive habits that can lead to a healthier, more fulfilling and balanced life. So, take a deep breath and embark on this journey, one simple habit at a time!

3. Let's Begin

This workbook allows you to focus on one new habit each week and reflect on your progress at the end of the week and year on whether the habit has been successfully integrated into your days. The goal is to continue as many habits as possible beyond their given week so they integrate into your life, as you adopt new ones. It would be challenging to adopt all 52 (though you can try), so just do your best. If you can adopt even 1, it will be beneficial for your health and well being. And through this journey always remember, excuses make today easier but, tomorrow harder.

The Wheel of Life is an excellent resource for gaining insights into achieving a more balanced life as we go on this journey.

Wheel of Life
Consider the following eight categories of life, add your own and assess each one on a scale from 1 to 10.

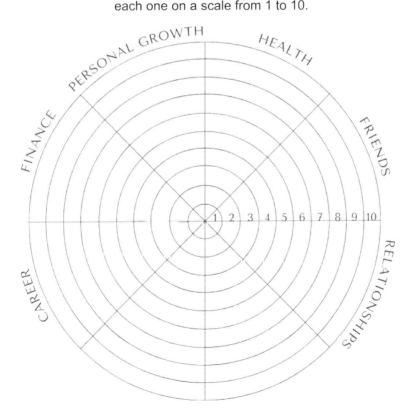

Week 1: Practice Deep Breathing

Why: *Reduces stress, lowers blood pressure, aids sleep and improves relaxation.*

Numerous studies, including a Northwestern University study found a strong link between breathing patterns and cognitive function, particularly during inhalation. Shallow breathing disrupts the oxygen and carbon dioxide balance in the body, leading to increased blood pressure and heart rate. Deep, longer breaths can counteract these effects by decreasing heart rate and blood pressure, thereby reducing cortisol, a stress hormone associated with aging. Additionally, shallow breathing limits the use of respiratory muscles, leading to decreased physical endurance and quicker fatigue. It can also contribute to sleep problems and exacerbate issues like headaches, neck, and upper back pain due to reduced engagement of the diaphragm.

Weekly Goal: Inhale and exhale 3-5 deep breaths before bed. Try to inhale, hold and exhale for as long as you can. If you can find other times of the day to practice deep breathing, even better.

Stacking Strategy: Immediately after you turn off the lights and are ready to drift, remember to take a moment to do your deep breaths.

Tips: You may want to put a sticky note on your light or bedside as a reminder. Follow a specific deep breathing pattern to help focus your mind and regulate your breath. One popular method is the 4-7-8 technique: inhale deeply through your nose for 4 seconds, hold your breath for 7 seconds, and then exhale slowly through your mouth for 8 seconds. This pattern helps to slow down your heart rate and promote relaxation.

TRACKER

WEEK OF: _____

MY GOALS	MY FEELINGS	DONE
Example: Put 1-3 goals for the week here	**Before/ During/ After:** hesitant, excited, effortless, energized, sluggish, silly, accomplished etc.	
MON		
TUES		
WED		
THURS		
FRI		
SAT		
SUN		

NOTES_____

Week 2: Drink More Water

Why: Enhances hydration, improves skin health, and aids digestion.

Water is essential for enhancing physical performance and endurance, promoting efficient digestion, and contributing to clearer, more hydrated skin. Additionally, adequate hydration is believed to improve cognitive functions and concentration, regulate body temperature effectively, and aid in weight management. These benefits highlight the importance of maintaining good hydration for overall health and well-being.

Weekly Goal: Drink a glass of water first thing in the morning, and ___ glasses throughout the day.

Stacking Strategy: There are so many activities throughout your day that this habit can be stacked on, including when you wake up. Below are more stacking tips you can use.

Tip: You can adopt one or more of these:
1. Morning Kickoff: Right after brushing your teeth, drink a glass of water; make it an extension of your morning routine.

2. Mealtime: Drink a glass of water before each meal. This not can also aid in digestion and potentially prevent overeating.

3. Work Breaks: Drink a glass of water each time you take a break i.e. after checking emails or when you stand up to stretch.

4. Evening Wind Down: After your evening activities, such as watching TV, reading, or cleaning up, have a glass of water before you start your bedtime routine.

Or forget all that, and simply have a water bottle at arms length all the time.

TRACKER

WEEK OF: _____

MY GOALS	MY FEELINGS	DONE
MON		
TUES		
WED		
THURS		
FRI		
SAT		
SUN		

NOTES_____
_____
_____
_____
_____
_____
_____
_____
_____
_____

Week 3: 2min Stretch

Why: Improves flexibility, reduces muscle tension, and enhances circulation. Plus it helps ground you.

If sitting or static for long periods, skipping regular stretching can increase the risk of muscle injuries and reduce flexibility, potentially leading to joint pain and a restricted range of motion. It also contributes to muscle stiffness and soreness, poor posture, and decreased blood circulation, which can affect overall well-being.

Weekly Goal: TwoMinute Stretch when you wake, mid morning and afternoon. Put in your phone timer so you don't forget.

Stacking Strategy: Drink a glass of water before or after stretching.

Tips: Have an alarm every 2 hours to remind you to stretch. Here is a quick set of stretches you can adopt that take just 2-minutes to complete.

1. **Standing Forward Bend (30 sec):** Targets hamstrings, calves, and back. Standing feet hip width apart, gently bend forward at the hips, and reach towards your toes. Hold for 30 seconds.
2. **Shoulder Shrugs and Rolls (30 sec):** Great for relieving tension in shoulders and neck. Raise shoulders up towards your ears, then roll them back and down. Do 10 reps.
3. **Side Stretch (30 sec):** Stand with your feet together, raise your arms overhead, clasp your hands, and gently lean to one side then switch to the other side. 15 seconds/ side.
4. **Chest Opener (30 sec):** Good if you sit at a desk all day. Stand or sit straight, clasp your hands behind your back, straighten your arms, and gently lift your hands upwards to stretch your chest. Hold for 30 seconds.
5. **Standing Quad Stretch (30 sec):** Stand on one foot, using a chair for balance if needed. Grab your other ankle and pull it towards your buttocks, keeping your knees close together. 15 sec./ side
6. **Neck Stretch (30 sec) :** Tilt your head to one side, bringing your ear close to the shoulder. Hold 15 seconds/ side.

TRACKER

WEEK OF: _____

MY GOALS	MY FEELINGS	DONE
MON		
TUES		
WED		
THURS		
FRI		
SAT		
SUN		

NOTES _____
_____
_____
_____
_____
_____
_____
_____
_____
_____
_____

Week 4: Practice Good Posture

Why: Reduces back pain, improves breathing, and enhances appearance.

Want to be a tad taller, then stand up straight! Over time you can lose up to 2" of height and age prematurely in appearance due to poor posture. Regularly practicing good posture and strengthening core and back muscles can help maintain spinal alignment and prevent height loss

Other problems that may arise from poor posture include chronic neck and back pain, core strength loss, potential spinal deformities, reduced lung capacity, joint wear and tear, impaired circulation, digestive problems, and an increased risk of cardiovascular issues.

Weekly Goal: Be mindful of and correct your posture throughout the day.

Stacking Strategy: Find different times in the day that can trigger as reminders. Right before eating, drinking water or stretching are good times to correct your posture.

Tips: A good tip for developing and maintaining a good posture habit is to set up your environment to encourage proper alignment. For instance, if you spend a lot of time sitting at a desk, ensure that your workspace is ergonomically arranged. Your chair should support your lower back, your feet should rest flat on the floor, and your computer screen should be at eye level to avoid leaning forward or looking down. Additionally, placing a small reminder note at your workspace or setting periodic reminders on your phone can prompt you to check and adjust your posture throughout the day. Regularly practicing exercises that strengthen your core muscles can also greatly contribute to maintaining good posture naturally.

TRACKER

WEEK OF: _____

MY GOALS	MY FEELINGS	DONE
MON		
TUES		
WED		
THURS		
FRI		
SAT		
SUN		

NOTES _____
_____
_____
_____
_____
_____
_____
_____
_____

Week 5: Journaling

Why: Increases positivity, reduces stress, improves mental wellbeing and forsters resilience.

Journaling can aid in processing emotions, organizing thoughts, enhancing self-awareness, and relieving stress. Without it, you may find it more challenging to reflect deeply on your experiences, track personal growth over time, or find a private outlet for emotional expression.

Weekly Goal: Just before bed, write down three things you're grateful for that day.

Stacking Strategy: Write these as you sip your evening glass of water. Keep a notebook at your bedside so it's always ready.

Tips: are some journaling prompts you could use to help get you started:

> Gratitude Reflection: "What are three things I am grateful for today and why? How do these things impact my life and my perspective on the world around me?"
>
> Overcoming Challenges: "What is one challenge I faced recently, and how did I overcome it? What did this experience teach me about my strengths and abilities?"
>
> Future Visualization: "Where do I see myself in five years, both personally and professionally? What steps can I take starting today to move closer to that vision?"

TRACKER

WEEK OF: _____

MY GOALS	MY FEELINGS	DONE
MON		
TUES		
WED		
THURS		
FRI		
SAT		
SUN		

NOTES_____

_____
_____
_____
_____
_____
_____
_____
_____
_____
_____

Week 6: Mindful Eating

Why: Promotes better digestion, enhances the enjoyment of meals, and helps in weight management.

Not practicing mindful eating can lead to overeating and potential weight gain due to a lack of awareness of fullness cues. It often results in diminished enjoyment and appreciation of meals, as well as poor digestion from eating too quickly. Furthermore, mindless eating can disconnect you from your body's natural hunger and satiety signals, potentially leading to unhealthy eating patterns and food choices.

Weekly Goal: Eat the first bite of a meal per day mindfully, focusing on the flavors, smells and textures.

Stacking Strategy: Before you begin eating, pause for a moment. Focus on your posture and consciously engage your senses.

Tips: For added impact, try closing your eyes on that first bite for a truly gastronomic experience.

> " Mindful eating replaces self-criticism with self-nurturing. It replaces shame with respect for your own inner wisdom.
> — Jan Chozen Bays "

TRACKER

WEEK OF: _____

MY GOALS	MY FEELINGS	DONE
MON		
TUES		
WED		
THURS		
FRI		
SAT		
SUN		

NOTES _____

Week 7: Daily Walking

Why: *Boosts cardiovascular health, improves mood, and increases energy levels.*

Missing out on this simple low-impact physical activity can contribute to poorer cardiovascular health and an increased risk of chronic diseases like heart disease and diabetes. Additionally, missing out on daily walks can lead to diminished mental health benefits, such as reduced stress relief, lower mood levels, and decreased cognitive function

Weekly Goal: Take a 5-15 minute walk every day, preferably after a meal.

Stacking Strategy: Keep your jacket and shoes ready to walk right after eating. During your walk you can practice good posture, and think about what you are grateful for, for writing before bed.

Tips: Incorporating a daily walking habit can be greatly beneficial for health, and here are three tips to make it a consistent part of your routine:

1. Set a Specific Time: Schedule your walks at a specific time each day, treating them like any important appointment. Consistency is key. Many people find success walking first thing in the morning, during a lunch break or after dinner.

2. Create Enjoyable Routes: Choose walking routes that you find enjoyable and varied. This could be a scenic path in a nearby park, a quiet neighborhood, or even a different part of your city.

3. Combine Walking with Other Activities: Make your walks more engaging by combining them with music, audiobooks or podcasts, or use this time to reflect and plan your day. You could also make it a social activity by inviting a friend or family member to join you.

TRACKER

WEEK OF: _____

MY GOALS	MY FEELINGS	DONE
MON		
TUES		
WED		
THURS		
FRI		
SAT		
SUN		

NOTES _____

Week 8: Improve Sleep Routine

Why: Enhances cognitive function, mood, and overall health.

Neglecting a consistent sleep routine can result in poor sleep quality and quantity, leading to fatigue, reduced cognitive function, and mood disturbances. Over time, irregular sleep patterns can increase the risk of health issues like obesity, heart disease, and diabetes. Establishing a regular sleep routine is crucial for overall health and well-being.

Weekly Goal: Establish a calm and consistent bedtime time.

Stacking Strategy: Incorporate your sleep routine with existing activities that signal to your body that it's time to sleep.

Tips: Lots of ways to adopt this through habit stacking.

- Dim lights in your home to create a calm atmosphere.
- Read a book for 10-15 minutes to relax your mind.
- Meditation or deep breathing exercises to reduce stress.
- Write in a journal gratitudes or thoughts to clear your thoughts.
- Doing gentle stretches or yoga poses to release physical tension.

> "It is a common experience that a problem difficult at night is resolved in the morning after the committee of sleep has worked on it.
> — John Steinbeck

TRACKER

WEEK OF: _____

MY GOALS	MY FEELINGS	DONE
MON		
TUES		
WED		
THURS		
FRI		
SAT		
SUN		

NOTES _____
_____
_____
_____
_____
_____
_____
_____
_____

Week 9: Decluttering

Why: *Creates a more organized environment, reduces stress, and improves focus.*

Neglecting to declutter can lead to increased stress and anxiety due to a chaotic environment. It can also decrease productivity and focus, as a cluttered space often hinders efficient workflow and clear thinking. Regular decluttering is essential for maintaining a peaceful and functional living or working space.

Weekly Goal: After dinner, spend 10 minutes a day decluttering a specific area of your home. Could be a room, a closet or even your car.

Stacking Strategy: Just before starting your night routine, start your 10-minute decluttering session. This can be done one specific day per week, or just after your walk or other habit.

Tips: Set a timer to 10-min for better chance of results. If inspired, keep going.

1. Start Small: Begin with a manageable area like a drawer or shelf to avoid feeling overwhelmed. Small victories can motivate you to tackle larger spaces.

2. Set Decluttering Goals: Define what you want to achieve with each decluttering session, whether it's clearing out a specific area or getting rid of a certain number of items.

3. Use the One-Year Rule: If you haven't used an item in a year, consider donating, selling, or discarding it. This rule helps in making decisions about what to keep and what to let go of.

4. Implement the Four-Box Method: One box for items to keep, one for donations, one for trash, and one for things you're unsure about. This method forces you to make a decision about each item and can significantly streamline the decluttering process. After finishing, deal with the contents of each box accordingly, and give yourself a timeframe to decide on the 'unsure' items.

TRACKER

WEEK OF: _____

MY GOALS	MY FEELINGS	DONE
MON		
TUES		
WED		
THURS		
FRI		
SAT		
SUN		

NOTES _____
_____
_____
_____
_____
_____
_____
_____
_____
_____

Week 10: Reduce Screen Time

Why: Decreases eye strain, improves sleep quality, and increases personal connection.

Excessive screen time can result in digital eye strain, sleep disturbances due to blue light exposure, and a more sedentary lifestyle, potentially leading to other health issues. It can also negatively impact mental health, contributing to anxiety, depression, and loneliness, especially from social media use. Moderating screen time is crucial for maintaining both physical and mental well-being.

Weekly Goal: In the morning schedule into your day 30 minutes without screen time. This includes text, social media, spotify/ apple play etc.

Stacking Strategy: Combine this with other habits like walking, meditation, deep breathing etc.

Tips: Reducing screen time can be challenging in our digitally connected world, but these three simple tips can help you cut down effectively:

1. Set Specific Screen-Free Times: Designate certain times of the day as screen-free. I.e. during meals, the first hour after waking up, or the hour before bedtime. Consistently can significantly reduce your overall screen exposure.

2. Use Screen Time Tracking Features: Many smartphones and digital devices now have built-in tools to track and limit screen time. Set daily limits for certain apps or overall usage.

3. Establish Screen-Free Zones: Create areas in your home, such as the bedroom or dining room, where screens are not allowed.

TRACKER

WEEK OF: _____

MY GOALS	MY FEELINGS	DONE
MON		
TUES		
WED		
THURS		
FRI		
SAT		
SUN		

NOTES _____
_____
_____
_____
_____
_____
_____
_____
_____
_____

Week 11: Healthy Snacking

Why: *Provides better nutrition, maintains energy levels, and helps in weight control.*

Unhealthy snacking can contribute to weight gain, blood sugar spikes, and poor nutrition, as snacks high in sugar, salt, and unhealthy fats lack essential nutrients. Incorporating healthy snacks is key for maintaining balanced energy levels throughout the day, managing hunger effectively, and ensuring a well-rounded diet.

Weekly Goal: Replace one unhealthy snack with a healthy option each day. Think about the time you usually snack, and then plan for it in advance for a better chance of success.

Stacking Strategy: Make that healthy snack in the morning while having your morning tea or coffee and planning out the day, so it's an easy option.

Tips: Here are three examples of simple yet satisfying snacks:

1. Apple Slices with Peanut Butter: Thinly sliced apples paired with a tablespoon of peanut butter offer a delightful mix of sweet and savory flavors, along with a good balance of fiber, healthy fats, and protein.

2. Greek Yogurt with Berries and Honey: A bowl of Greek yogurt topped with fresh berries and a drizzle of honey provides a creamy texture with natural sweetness, packed with protein and antioxidants.

3. Hummus with Carrot and Cucumber Sticks: This is a crunchy, hydrating, and protein-rich snack. The creamy hummus with the crispness of carrot and cucumber sticks makes for a satisfying and nutritious option.

TRACKER

WEEK OF: _____

MY GOALS	MY FEELINGS	DONE
MON		
TUES		
WED		
THURS		
FRI		
SAT		
SUN		

NOTES _____

Week 12: Oil Pulling

Why: *Believed to enhance oral health, whiten teeth, and improve overall well being.*

Apparently this gets your teeth sparkly white! Oil pulling, a recent trend but also an ancient Ayurvedic dental technique, helps reduce bacteria in the mouth, particularly Streptococcus mutans known to cause tooth decay, reduce plaque buildup and lower the risk of tartar formation, whiten teeth, promote healthier gums, and may help in reducing bad breath. While scientific backing is minimal, this is an ancient technique that at worst will improve your breath.

Weekly Goal: Commit to oil pulling for 5-10 minutes each morning before breakfast or when convenient.

Stacking Strategy: Do daily while listening to a morning news podcast, planning your day, or preparing your breakfast (if it doesn't require too much talking!).

Tips: Here is a simple process that doesn't require a complex recipe:

- Ingredients: High-quality oil (commonly used oils include coconut oil, sesame oil, or sunflower oil).
- Keep a cup nearby in case someone wants to talk to you.
- Spit into trash since it can clog your sink

Instructions:

1. Oil: Coconut oil is popular due to its pleasant taste and antimicrobial properties. Sesame and sunflower oil are also traditional choices.
2. Quantity: Use about one tablespoon of oil. Oil will liquify in your mouth.
3. Swishing: Place the oil in your mouth and gently swish the oil around your mouth, through your teeth and around your gums. Do this for about 5-10 minutes or longer if you can.
4. Disposal: After swishing, spit the oil into a trash can. Avoid spitting it into the sink or toilet as it can solidify, especially if you're using coconut oil.
5. Remember, while many people report benefits from oil pulling, it's a complementary practice and not a substitute for professional dental care.

TRACKER

WEEK OF: _____

MY GOALS	MY FEELINGS	DONE
MON		
TUES		
WED		
THURS		
FRI		
SAT		
SUN		

NOTES _____
_____
_____
_____
_____
_____
_____
_____

Week 13: Morning Meditation

Why: *Enhances mental clarity, reduces anxiety, and improves emotional health.*

If you skip your morning meditation, you might miss out on the peaceful start to the day it provides. Without this centering practice, your day could feel more stressful and less focused, potentially leading to a sense of disarray in your daily routine. While these effects are subtle, they highlight the gentle, yet powerful, impact of your morning meditation in setting a positive tone for your day.

Weekly Goal: Meditate for 5-10 minutes each morning when you first wake.

Stacking Strategy: As soon as you wake up and are still in bed, begin your meditation practice. This ensures that meditation is the first activity of your day, setting a positive and mindful tone.

Tips: Sit or lay in bed on your back, hands on your belly, focus on your breath and then scan each part of your body slowly from your toes to the top of your head. Here are some things to keep in mind:

1. Comfortable Position: Sit or lie in a comfortable spot with a straight back. Relax your hands and neck.

2. Focus on Breath: Breathe deeply and slowly, paying attention to the sensation of breathing. If distracted, gently return focus to your breath.

3. Embrace Wandering Thoughts: When your mind wanders, acknowledge it without judgment and refocus on your breathing. Remember, practice and patience are key.

Meditation is a skill that develops over time. Be patient with yourself and enjoy the journey of becoming more mindful and centered. If legal in your area, a microdose of cannabis (1mg) or CBD (5-10mg) can assist you in learning how to meditate in the beginning. Do your research and speak to a health professional.

TRACKER

WEEK OF: _____

MY GOALS	MY FEELINGS	DONE
MON		
TUES		
WED		
THURS		
FRI		
SAT		
SUN		

NOTES _____
_____
_____
_____
_____
_____
_____
_____
_____
_____

Week 14: Morning Affirmations

Why: Boosts self-esteem, counters negative thoughts, positive mindset and motivates for success.

Weekly Goal: Write down 1-3 positive affirmations, and read them each morning or meditate on them.

Stacking Strategy: Monday, right after you complete your morning hygiene routine, such as brushing your teeth or washing your face, take a moment to write down your affirmations. The rest of the week use your morning meditation as a time to reflect on your affirmations.

Tips: Here are five examples you can use or create your own:

1. "Today, I choose to see the best in everything and everyone around me."This affirmation sets a tone of positivity and openness, encouraging you to look for the good in your day.

2. "I am capable, strong, and worthy of all the good that comes my way." - This affirmation boosts self-esteem and confidence. It reminds you of your inner strength and your deservingness of positive experiences.

3. "Each challenge I face is an opportunity to grow and learn." - This affirmation helps frame any difficulties or obstacles as a chance for personal development, fostering a growth mindset.

4. "With every breath, I release the stress of yesterday and focus on the potential of today." - This affirmation is about letting go of past worries and focusing on the present, embracing the new day with hope and optimism.

5. "I possess the strength, courage, and wisdom to handle anything that comes my way today." - This affirmation reinforces self-confidence and resilience, empowering you to face the day's tasks and uncertainties with assurance.

TRACKER

WEEK OF: _____

MY GOALS	MY FEELINGS	DONE
MON		
TUES		
WED		
THURS		
FRI		
SAT		
SUN		

NOTES _____
_____
_____
_____
_____
_____
_____
_____
_____
_____
_____

Week 15: Morning Phone Detox

Why: *Not checking your phone first thing can enhance mental clarity and reduce stress.*

Have you ever had your morning disappear because you went into the cell-phone void? Checking your phone first thing can disrupt your initial state of calm and focus, and eat away at time without you realizing. This habit often leads to an immediate influx of information and distractions, which can overwhelm your brain and hinder your ability to prioritize and plan effectively. It can also increase stress and anxiety levels by exposing you to potential stressors right away, setting a tense tone for the day. Additionally, this practice can detract from morning productivity, as it often leads to getting sidetracked from important morning routines or new habits.

Weekly Goal: Go the entire week without checking your phone until at least 10-30 minutes after you wake.

Stacking Strategy: When you wake, don't check your phone until after meditation, your morning routine or eating a healthy breakfast.

Tips: To avoid the temptation of checking your phone first thing in the morning, consider these three tips:

1. Create a morning routine that doesn't involve your phone. This could include activities like meditation, reading, exercising, or simply enjoying a quiet cup of coffee. This can help you start the day calmly and with intention.

2. Designate specific times for checking your phone in the morning, ideally after you've completed your morning routine. Scheduling a set time to check your phone, you can manage your time and attention more effectively..

3. Establish a designated "no-phone zone" in your bedroom. Keep your phone outside of the bedroom or place it on a charging station away from your bed to reduce temptation.

TRACKER

WEEK OF: _____

MY GOALS	MY FEELINGS	DONE
MON		
TUES		
WED		
THURS		
FRI		
SAT		
SUN		

NOTES _____
_____
_____
_____
_____
_____
_____
_____
_____
_____

Week 16: Night Time Phone Detox

Why: Improves mental well-being, sex life, sleep quality and physical health and decreases anxiety, stress.

Using your phone before bed can hinder your ability to fall asleep. The blue light from the screen disrupts melatonin production, delaying sleep onset. Engaging with stimulating content keeps your mind active, increasing stress and making relaxation difficult. This habit can lead to a cycle of difficulty in falling asleep, affecting your overall sleep quality.

Weekly Goal: Put your phone away 15-30 minutes before you sleep.

Stacking Strategy: Replace this bad habit with those that improve your sleep and reduce stress, such as reading, meditation, journaling or stretching.

Tips: Make it a habit to put away just before brushing your teeth, i.e. Minty breath = no phone, nacks, sugary drinks etc.

And re-use tips recommended for Morning Phone Detox, week 15.

TRACKER

WEEK OF: _____

MY GOALS	MY FEELINGS	DONE
MON		
TUES		
WED		
THURS		
FRI		
SAT		
SUN		

NOTES _____
_____
_____
_____
_____
_____
_____
_____
_____
_____

Week 17: Practice Kindness

***Why:** Increases happiness, reduces stress, and builds positive social connections.*

Acts of kindness release happiness-inducing hormones, strengthen relationships, and encourage empathy. Kindness is contagious and can lead to positive social change. It enhances resilience, promotes optimism, and contributes to a more compassionate and inclusive society. In essence, kindness is a universal currency that enriches lives and has the power to transform individuals and communities for the better.

Weekly Goal: Perform one act of kindness each day. Can be as simple as a warm thank you or compliment to a stranger or a call to someone in need. Make it intentional. It takes 2.5 seconds to send a short message.

Stacking Strategy: Each evening right before brushing your teeth send a kind message to someone.

Tips: Here are five sample texts to express kindness:

- For a Friend: "Hi [Friend's Name], I've been thinking about how lucky I am to have you in my life. Thanks for always being there for me!"

- For a Family Member: "Hey [Family Member's Name], just a quick message to say thank you for always being my rock. Your love and support mean the world to me. I'm so grateful for you!"

- For a Colleague: "Hello [Colleague's Name], I wanted to express my gratitude for your help with [specific project/task]. Your expertise and willingness to assist made a huge difference. Thank you!"

- For a Mentor/ Teacher: "Dear [Mentor/Teacher's Name], I am so grateful for the guidance and wisdom you've shared with me. Your mentorship has been invaluable in my growth. Thank you for everything!"

- General Gratitude: "Hi [Name], just a note to say how much I appreciate you and everything you do. Your kindness and generosity don't go unnoticed. Thank you for being amazing!"

TRACKER

WEEK OF: _____

MY GOALS	MY FEELINGS	DONE
MON		
TUES		
WED		
THURS		
FRI		
SAT		
SUN		

NOTES _____

Week 18: Read Before Bed

Why: *Reduces stress, improves brain function, and enhances sleep quality.*

Reading before bed helps in winding down after a busy day, reducing stress levels and promoting better sleep. Engaging in a book or a calming story can transport your mind to a different world, easing you into a state of relaxation. Additionally, the absence of screens reduces exposure to blue light, aiding in the production of melatonin, the sleep hormone.

Weekly Goal: Read a book or kindle for 10 minutes before bed each night. Do not read from your phone, the blue light and stimulation is counter to this good habit.

Stacking Habit: Right before brushing your teeth and sending a kind message, trade your phone for a book.

Tips: Make your bedside area comfortable with soft lighting, a comfortable chair or pillows, a warm blanket and your book ready. Having a cozy reading nook makes it more appealing to settle in with a book before sleep, turning it into a comforting nightly ritual.

> "The more that you read, the more things you will know. The more that you learn, the more places you'll go."
> — Dr. Seuss

TRACKER

WEEK OF: _____

MY GOALS	MY FEELINGS	DONE
MON		
TUES		
WED		
THURS		
FRI		
SAT		
SUN		

NOTES _____

Week 19: Do something Uncomfortable

Why: *Fosters personal growth, resilience, confidence, creativity, and can lead to the discovery of new interests and passions.*

Avoiding uncomfortable situations may result in missed opportunities for growth, personal stagnation, and limited resilience. Stepping out of your comfort zone can lead to valuable learning experiences and achievements. Refusing discomfort can also erode self-confidence and result in regrets over missed chances. While it's natural to seek comfort, it's important to strike a balance by occasionally embracing discomfort, as it often serves as a catalyst for personal and professional development, ultimately enriching your life journey.

Weekly Goal: Try something uncomfortable every day.

Stacking Strategy: Cold shower after morning stretch, deep breathing before engaging in activity, journaling the experience or uncomfortable activities you want to challenge.

Tips: Uncomfortable activities to consider:

- Public Speaking: Many people find speaking in front of a crowd daunting, but it's a valuable skill for personal and professional development.
- Networking: Attending networking events can be intimidating but is crucial for career growth.
- Learning a New Skill: Be it dance, a new language or a musical instrument, starting from scratch can be challenging.
- Physical Challenges: Like cold plunging, running or hiking a tough trail, physical challenges push your limits.
- Asking for Feedback: Actively seeking constructive criticism can be uncomfortable but is vital for improvement.

TRACKER

WEEK OF: _____

MY GOALS	MY FEELINGS	DONE
MON		
TUES		
WED		
THURS		
FRI		
SAT		
SUN		

NOTES _____
_____
_____
_____
_____
_____
_____
_____
_____
_____
_____

Week 20: Early Morning Rise

Why: Increases productivity, provides quiet time, and improves time management.

Waking up just 15 minutes earlier each day may seem like a minor adjustment, however this extra time offers a peaceful start to your morning, allowing you to set a positive tone for the day. It's a small investment in time that pays significant dividends in your daily life and overall well-being.

Weekly Goal: Wake up just 10-15 minutes earlier than usual at least one day per week and increase with time.

Stacking Strategy: You can use it to plan, savor a leisurely breakfast, engage in a short mindfulness practice, or simply enjoy a moment of calm before the rush begins.

Tips: Set your alarm 15 min earlier and plan a specific, enjoyable or motivating activity to do as soon as you wake up, such as meditation, affirmations or stretching. Over time, these 15 minutes add up, giving you the equivalent of extra weeks or even months of productive time over the course of a year.

> "Morning is an important time of day because how you spend your morning can often tell you what kind of day you are going to have."
> — Lemony Snicket

TRACKER

WEEK OF: _____

MY GOALS	MY FEELINGS	DONE
MON		
TUES		
WED		
THURS		
FRI		
SAT		
SUN		

NOTES_____
_____
_____
_____
_____
_____
_____
_____
_____
_____
_____

Week 21: Sugar Free Day

***Why:** Improves health, reduces risk of diseases, and enhances energy levels.*

Weekly Goal: Avoid sugary snacks and drinks every Monday and try to make it to Sunday.

Stacking Strategy: Mindful eating, healthy snacks, focus on posture or drink water before snacking as a reminder to avoid sugars

Tips: A successful approach to having a sugar-free day is to incorporate it into your routine of grocery shopping and meal planning. Here's a structured plan:

- During Grocery Shopping: Make it a habit to buy no sugary healthy snacks. This sets you up for success by ensuring you have the right foods at home.
- Meal Prep and Planning: When planning your meals for the week, specifically design your Monday's menu (and the rest of the week, if possible) to be sugar-free. Plan each meal and snack to avoid the temptation of reaching for sugary options.
- Mindful Eating on Mondays: On Mondays, be particularly mindful of your eating choices. Start your day with a reminder of your sugar-free goal. You could put a note on the fridge or set a reminder on your phone.
- Gradual Extension: Once you get comfortable with sugar-free Mondays, gradually extend this habit to other days gradually reducing sugar intake.

TRACKER

WEEK OF: _____

MY GOALS	MY FEELINGS	DONE
MON		
TUES		
WED		
THURS		
FRI		
SAT		
SUN		

NOTES _____

Week 22: Have a Buddha Smile

Why: *Enhance mood, reduce stress and anxiety, promote mindfulness, improve social connections, boost immune function and foster a positive mental attitude. May also prevents jowls from sagging down (grumpy face).*

While there may not be specific research or statistics on the Buddha smile, its significance is rooted in ancient teachings and practices. When practiced, it is believed to reduce stress, elevate mood, and enhance overall well-being. Additionally, the Buddha smile fosters social connections and reminds individuals to stay present and cultivate inner peace. While its impact may not be quantifiable, its value lies in promoting emotional well-being, positive interactions, and a more mindful and serene approach to life.

Weekly Goal: Maintain a soft, serene, contented, and mindful smile throughout the day, even when alone at your computer.

Stacking Strategy: Pair with regular daily activities.

Tips: Smile gently as soon as you wake up and right before you go to sleep. This sets a positive tone for your day and a peaceful mindset for your night. Other moments to practice this habit:

1. **During Transition:** Use daily transitions as cues to smile. These could be moments like after finishing a task, before starting a new one, or when moving from one room to another.

2. **Before & After Meals:** Smile softly before beginning to eat and once you've finished your meal. This not only promotes mindfulness but also enhances the enjoyment of your food.

3. **While Interacting with Others:** Practice smiling during conversations, whether it's in person or over a call. This not only improves your mood but also positively affects your social interactions.

TRACKER

WEEK OF: _____

MY GOALS	MY FEELINGS	DONE
MON		
TUES		
WED		
THURS		
FRI		
SAT		
SUN		

NOTES_____

Week 23: Conscious Breathing

Why: Reduces anxiety, improves focus, and aids in relaxation.

Research has shown that conscious breathing can significantly reduce stress levels, with studies indicating decreases in cortisol, the stress hormone, after mindful breathing sessions. Moreover, conscious breathing enhances cognitive function, improving attention, memory, and problem-solving skills. Studies have also demonstrated its effectiveness in reducing symptoms of anxiety and depression as found in a study published in the Journal of Clinical Psychology. Overall, the evidence suggests that conscious breathing is a scientifically validated practice that can reduce stress, improve mental health, and enhance cognitive function.

Weekly Goal: Practice conscious breathing exercises for 5 -10 breaths daily at any time. This involves focusing your attention on the process of inhaling and exhaling

Stacking Strategy: Could practice while waiting in line, right before a meal, during yoga or a walk or while meditating.

Tips: For as long as you are alive your breath is always there, so this is an easy habit to come back to time and time again.

Use reminders and incorporate it into daily activities, such as taking deep breaths before meals or during moments of waiting.

- Deep breaths in stressful situations can help maintain calm.
- Guided meditation apps and accountability from a friend can provide support and structure.
- Keep a journal to track your progress

Remember that consistency takes time, so be patient and compassionate with yourself.

TRACKER

WEEK OF: _____

MY GOALS	MY FEELINGS	DONE
MON		
TUES		
WED		
THURS		
FRI		
SAT		
SUN		

NOTES _____
_____
_____
_____
_____
_____
_____
_____
_____
_____

Week 24: Morning Sun Salutation

Why: *Increases flexibility, reduces stress, and improves mental focus.*

The practice of morning sun salutation, known as Surya Namaskar in yoga, offers an energizing start to the day by boosting vitality and alertness through a combination of stretching and strengthening exercises. Beyond its physical benefits, sun salutations promote mindfulness and mental clarity, reducing stress and anxiety. This practice also contributes to improved posture, digestive health, and the establishment of a consistent morning routine, fostering discipline and motivation.

Weekly Goal: Do 3 rounds as soon as you wake, facing east if possible. It will take less than 3 minutes. You can replace 2 min stretches with this practice or combine.

Stacking Strategy: Practice with conscious breathing, meditation or affirmation habits.

Tips: Don't ask yourself if you feel like it, just roll out of bed in your pajamas, eyes closed and begin. And just use the floor, keep it low maintenance for a better chance of success. Remind yourself that it takes less than 3 minutes as a motivating factor.

There are many variations of Morning Sun Salutation, the one shown in the upcoming page is one of the most basic. It was selected for this reason, because its simplicity makes it easier to adopt as a long-term habit. Stick to this one as a baseline, and on days when you feel inspired you can always add more poses.

It's important to synchronize your breath with your movements in each pose for the full benefit. Inhale as you expand or stretch, and exhale as you contract or fold.

TRACKER

WEEK OF: _____

MY GOALS	MY FEELINGS	DONE
MON		
TUES		
WED		
THURS		
FRI		
SAT		
SUN		

NOTES _____

Morning Sun Salutation

Here is a sample variation

Mountain Pose
Stand with your feet together, arms by your side. Inhale and extend your arms overhead, palms facing each other.

Forward Fold
Exhale and bend forward from your hips, not your waist. Bring your hands down to touch the floor beside your feet.

1/2 Standing Forward Fold
Inhale and lift your torso halfway up, lengthening your spine. Your back should be flat, and fingertips should be on the ground or your shins.

Plank Pose
Exhale and step or jump into a plank position. Keep your body in a straight line from your heels to your head. Inhale to low plank down to floor, elbows close to your body.

Upward Facing Dog
Inhale and straighten your arms, pushing your chest forward and up. Lift your thighs off the floor, only your hands and tops of the feet on the ground.

Downward Facing Dog
Exhale and lift your hips up and back, forming an inverted V shape. Keep your hands shoulder-width apart and feet hip-width apart.

Repeat your way back to Mountain Pose: Inhaling to 1/2 Standing Forward Fold, exhale to to Forward Pose, inhale to Mountain Pose to complete this round. Repeat 2 more times.

Illustrated by River Robinson

Week 25: Take the Stairs

Why: *Using stairs burns calories, strengthens muscles, improves cardiovascular health and is associated with longevity.*

Research in Blue Zones, regions known for the longevity of their residents, supports the idea that physical activity, including activities like taking the stairs and going up and down hills contributes to longer and healthier lives. Studies conducted in Blue Zones, such as Okinawa, Japan, and Sardinia, Italy, have consistently found that daily movement, in the form of walking, climbing stairs, and other routine physical activities, is a common practice among these long-lived populations. It is considered a key factor in their exceptional life expectancy. These studies emphasize that incorporating physical activity into daily life, even in small ways like using stairs, can have a significant impact on health and longevity, aligning with the notion that a simple change in behavior can lead to substantial benefits over time.

Weekly Goal: From now on, take the Stairs Instead of the Elevator when possible.

Stacking Strategy: Incorporate breathing, posture and water intake.

Tips: Associate the action of taking stairs with your regular practice of entering or leaving buildings. Turn it into a natural part of your routine. Remind yourself of the benefits.

TRACKER

WEEK OF: _____

MY GOALS	MY FEELINGS	DONE
MON		
TUES		
WED		
THURS		
FRI		
SAT		
SUN		

NOTES _____

Week 26: Mid-Year Reflection

Why: *Offers perspective, assesses progress, and re-aligns goals.*

A mid-year reflection acts as a powerful tool for personal growth, enabling you to step back and view the bigger picture of your achievements and challenges. By reviewing and acknowledging your successes, you reinforce positive behaviors and gain motivation. Simultaneously, recognizing and understanding your challenges provides critical learning opportunities. This process of introspection ensures that your goals remain relevant and aligned with your evolving aspirations and circumstances, making it a pivotal moment in your year-long journey of self-improvement.

Weekly Goal: Review the past 25 weeks and reflect on your growth and challenges. Write down 3 wins and 3 challenges.

Stacking Strategy: Combine this with your weekly planning or journaling routine to integrate reflection naturally.

Tips: Here's a journaling outline with questions and answers (Q&A) format for your mid-year reflection in a 52-week habit journey:

1. Habit Review

From the habits from Week 1 to Week 25, which ones have you successfully integrated into your routine?

Which habits did you find challenging to maintain? Why?

2. Successes and Challenges

What are your top three successes in these first 26 weeks?

Describe three major challenges you faced. How did you address them?

3. Personal Growth

In what ways have you noticed personal growth or change since beginning this journey?

Have there been any unexpected benefits or learnings from this process?

4. Adjustments for Future Weeks

Based on your experience so far, what adjustments would you like to make for the upcoming weeks?

Are there any habits you feel you need to revisit or focus more on?

5. Setting Goals

What specific goals do you want to achieve in the next 26 weeks?

How will you modify your approach to these habits based on your learnings?

What motivates you to continue on this journey?

Write a motivational note to yourself for the days you might struggle.

Additional thoughts, reflections or words of encouragement to self.

TRACKER

WEEK OF: _____

MY GOALS	MY FEELINGS	DONE
MON		
TUES		
WED		
THURS		
FRI		
SAT		
SUN		

NOTES _____
_____
_____
_____
_____
_____
_____
_____
_____

Week 27: Create a Vision Board

Why: Helps in visualizing your goals, serving as a constant source of inspiration and motivation.

Psychological studies have shown that visualizing a goal can be almost as powerful as the actual practice in terms of enhancing performance and motivation. Vision boards could serve as a tool for such visualization, constantly reminding individuals of their goals and aspirations. Without a vision board, you might find it easier to lose track of your commitments and less likely to hold yourself accountable for progress towards your goals.

Weekly Goal: Set aside time this week to create a vision board for your future goals. This can be done 1-2 times per year to align with your evolving goals and aspirations.

Stacking Strategy: Tie in with your regular goal-setting or reflection sessions. Alternatively, pair it with a creative hobby or a relaxed weekend afternoon when you can dedicate time.

Tips: You can create a digital Vision Board using tools such as Canva, Pintrest or Adobe Spark or a physical Vision Board using a board, paper and magazines. Here's a quick step-by-step guide to making your own:

1. Define Your Goals and Aspirations: Start by reflecting on what you want to achieve in different areas of your life - career, personal growth, relationships, health, hobbies, travel, etc. Think about both short-term and long-term goals.

2. Gather Materials: For a physical board, you'll need a board (like alarge poster board), magazines, printouts, photos, scissors, glue or pins, and markers or pens.

3. Find Visual Representations: Seek images, words, quotes, and symbols that resonate with your goals and aspirations. These should evoke positive emotions and be closely aligned with what you want.

4. Create a Layout: Before you start gluing or pinning items to your board, arrange them on the board to get an idea of the layout. You

might group items by theme or spread them out evenly. Consider leaving some space for future additions.

5. Add Personal Touches: Feel free to write or draw on your vision board, adding dates, affirmations, or specific goals.

6. Display Your Vision Board: Place your vision board somewhere you'll see it regularly, like your screen saver or phone if it's digital, and bedroom, office, or another personal space is physical. The idea is to keep your goals visually and mentally present in your everyday life.

7. Update Regularly: Your goals and aspirations might change or evolve, so feel free to update your vision board as needed. It's a living representation of your aspirations.

TRACKER

WEEK OF: _____

MY GOALS	MY FEELINGS	DONE
MON		
TUES		
WED		
THURS		
FRI		
SAT		
SUN		

Week 28: Nighttime Routine

Why: Enhances sleep quality, reduces stress, and prepares the body for rest.

Consistency in sleep patterns can align your body's internal clock, promoting a healthier sleep schedule. Quality sleep not only enhances cognitive function and productivity but also contributes to better mental and physical health. Moreover, a bedtime routine offers personal time for self-care and can strengthen relationships. In the long term, it fosters a healthier lifestyle and supports longevity.

Weekly Goal: Establish a calming nighttime routine.

Stacking Strategy: Could include many of the habits from previous weeks, a cup of tea, goodnight wishes to family, journaling, meditation or a book. Review past weeks and see if there are any habits you'd like to incorporate.

Tips: Here are five concise tips to help you establish and maintain a bedtime routine:

1. Set a Consistent Bedtime: Choose a specific time to go to bed each night, weekends excluded for now.

2. Create a Relaxing Pre-Bedtime Routine: Include calming activities like reading, meditation, or gentle stretching in the hour before bedtime to signal your body it's time to wind down.

3. Limit Screen Time: Avoid screens (phones, tablets, computers) at least an hour before bed to reduce the impact of blue light on your sleep.

4. Prepare Your Sleep Environment: Make your bedroom comfortable, dark, and cool to optimize sleep quality.

5. Stay Active During the Day: Engage in regular physical activity, but aim to finish exercise a few hours before bedtime to avoid stimulation.

TRACKER

WEEK OF: _____

MY GOALS	MY FEELINGS	DONE
MON		
TUES		
WED		
THURS		
FRI		
SAT		
SUN		

NOTES_____

Week 29: Fast After Dinner

Why: *Can improve digestion and sleep quality, aid in weight management, regulate blood sugar levels, reduce risk of acid reflux and promote healthier eating habits.*

Ready to boost your health while you sleep? Studies suggest that nighttime fasting can be beneficial for metabolic health, weight loss, cardiovascular health, and inflammation reduction.A pivotal study at the Salk Institute for Biological Studies, published in "Cell Metabolism," found that nighttime fasting led to significant improvements in metabolic health. Participants experienced notable weight and body fat reduction. Another study featured in the "Journal of the American College of Cardiology" established a link between nighttime fasting and a reduced risk of coronary artery disease and diabetes, showcasing the cardiovascular benefits of this eating pattern.

Weekly Goal: Skip snacking after dinner and fast until morning.

Stacking Strategy: Incorporate it into your sleep routine and eat a healthy breakfast in the morning.

Tips: Fasting after dinner involves refraining from eating any food from dinner time until breakfast the next morning. Here's how to practice it and what it generally entails for best results:

1. Define Your Fasting Window: Decide on a specific time frame to start a 10-14 hour fast. This means if you finish dinner at 7 PM, you don't eat again until 7 AM the next day.

2. Be Consistent: Consistency is key for reaping the benefits of fasting. Try to stick to your fasting schedule as closely as possible each day.

3. Break the Fast Gently: When you break your fast in the morning, start with a light and nutritious meal.

TRACKER

WEEK OF: _____

MY GOALS	MY FEELINGS	DONE
MON		
TUES		
WED		
THURS		
FRI		
SAT		
SUN		

NOTES_____
_____
_____
_____
_____
_____
_____
_____
_____
_____

Week 30: Explore Nature

Why: *Boosts mood, enhances creativity, and provides a sense of calm and grounding.*

Research has shown that spending time in nature reduces stress, improves mental and physical health, enhances cognitive function and creativity, while a lack of nature exposure can negatively impact mental health and increase feelings of stress and isolation.

Weekly Goal: Visit a natural setting and spend time exploring or work in your garden even in cold months

Stacking Strategy: Enjoy nature during your 10 min walk, while writing a letter or thoughtful messages, journaling or during mindful breathing

Tips: Here are several tips to help you include time in nature as part of a new habit:

1. Schedule Nature Time: Just like any important appointment, schedule specific times for outdoor activities in your calendar. This could be a weekend hike, a morning garden session, or an evening walk. Treating these moments as fixed appointments increases the likelihood of following through.

2. Create a Morning or Evening Routine: Incorporate nature into your morning or evening routine. Have your coffee outside, practice yoga in a park, or enjoy reading a book under a tree.

3. Join a Group or Club: Crate or participate in outdoor groups or clubs, such as hiking, bird watching, or gardening clubs, can provide motivation and social interaction, making the habit more enjoyable and sustainable.

4. Use Nature as a Workout Setting: Replace gym workouts with outdoor activities. This could be jogging, cycling, or doing bodyweight exercises in a park. It adds the benefit of fresh air and natural scenery to your fitness routine.

5. Involve Family or Friends: Turn your nature time into a social activity. Plan regular outdoor family outings or meet friends for walks instead

of indoor gatherings. This adds a social incentive to your nature habit.

6. Mindfulness in Nature: Practice mindfulness or meditation in a natural setting. This can heighten the experience and create a powerful, peaceful habit of connecting with the outdoors.

7. Digital Detox in Nature: Designate time in nature as a period to disconnect from digital devices. This can enhance your connection with the natural environment and make the experience more rejuvenating.

TRACKER

WEEK OF: _____

MY GOALS	MY FEELINGS	DONE
MON		
TUES		
WED		
THURS		
FRI		
SAT		
SUN		

NOTES _____

Week 31: Learn Something New

Why: *Keeps the brain active, fosters curiosity, and builds new skills.*

Stay sharp! Overall, the process of learning new things keeps the brain and body active and engaged, fostering a healthier and more fulfilling life. Cognitively, it stimulates the brain, enhancing neuroplasticity, which can improve memory and delay cognitive decline associated with aging. This mental engagement has been linked to a lower risk of dementia and Alzheimer's disease. Emotionally, learning new skills can boost self-esteem and increase life satisfaction, leading to better mental health and reduced symptoms of depression and anxiety. New physical skills can improve motor skills, coordination, and general physical health.Weekly Goal: Spend time each day or a specific week day learning a new skill or topic.

Stacking Strategy: You could stack with your reading habit, as part of cooking healthy meals or when doing something uncomfortable.

Weekly Goal: Journal at least one new thing you learn each day this week and think of something you would aspire to start learning in the coming year.

Tips: Here are samples of activities that not only enrich your skill set but also offer mental, emotional, and physical benefits:

1. Language Learning: Picking up a new language not only enhances cognitive skills but also opens up opportunities to explore new cultures and connect with more people.

2. Musical Instrument: Learning to play an instrument is known to improve memory and concentration.

3. Art and Craft: Exploring creative skills such as painting, DIY, drawing, pottery, or knitting can be therapeutic and a great outlet for self-expression.

4. Cooking or Baking: Mastering new recipes or cooking techniques not only is enjoyable but also leads to healthier eating habits.

5. Gardening: Gardening gives you a chance to learn about different plants and relax with nature.

6. Writing: Whether it's creative writing, journaling, or blogging, writing enhances communication skills and offers a medium for self-reflection and creativity.

7. Dance, Martial Arts or Yoga: These disciplines not only improve physical fitness but also teach important principles like discipline, patience, and mindfulness.

8. Investing and Finance Management: Understanding the basics of investing, budgeting, and financial management is crucial for long-term financial health.

TRACKER

WEEK OF: _____

MY GOALS	MY FEELINGS	DONE
MON		
TUES		
WED		
THURS		
FRI		
SAT		
SUN		

Week 32: Write a Letter

Why Encourages thoughtful communication, strengthens relationships, and fosters nostalgia.

Research in the "Journal of Happiness Studies" found that writing letters, like thank you notes, boosts happiness and life satisfaction. Therapeutically, as shown in studies by the "American Psychological Association," letter writing aids in processing emotions in situations like grief. Overall, these findings suggest that letter writing is beneficial for mental health, emotional processing, and strengthening connections with others.

Weekly Goal: Write a letter to a friend or family member. This can be a weekly or monthly goal moving forward.

Stacking Strategy: Write during your fast and evening routine or after morning.

Tips: Find a quiet, pensive time and space in your home. You could use your leisurely weekend morning coffee time or a calm evening. Alternatively, if you already set aside time for journaling or weekly planning, include letter writing once a week or month. Here are some ideas to help you get started:

- Gratitude Letter: Write about someone who has made a significant impact on your life. Describe how they influenced you and express your gratitude.
- Memory Sharing: Share a fond memory you have with the recipient of your letter. Describe the details of this memory and why it's special to you.
- A Letter to Your Past Self: Write a letter to yourself at a younger age. Offer advice, reassurances, or reflections on how your life has progressed.
- A Letter to Your Future Self: Write a letter to yourself in the future. Describe your current life, feelings, and hopes for what you will have achieved by then.
- Offering Support: If the recipient is going through a challenging time, offer words of support and encouragement. Share your own experiences if they're relevant and might provide comfort.

TRACKER

WEEK OF: _____

MY GOALS	MY FEELINGS	DONE
MON		
TUES		
WED		
THURS		
FRI		
SAT		
SUN		

NOTES _____

Week 33: Express Gratitude

Why: Increases happiness, builds resilience, and strengthens relationships.

Gratitude boosts overall happiness and life satisfaction, with research indicating that individuals who regularly express gratitude report feeling happier. Moreover, gratitude strengthens social bonds, improving relationship satisfaction. Physically, grateful individuals often experience fewer health issues and better sleep quality, as highlighted in various health studies. Gratitude promotes mental well-being, enhancing relationships, and contributing to long-term physical health.

Weekly Goals: Express gratitude to someone or yourself each day.

Stacking Strategy: This can be part of your meditation, stretching/ yoga, deep breathing, while you enjoy a glass of water, during morning affirmation, journaling, writing letters or texting.

Tips: Often, the most meaningful acts are simple, thoughtful gestures that show care and compassion to those around you. Here are some concepts to help you find gratitude:

People in Your Life: Reflect on the individuals who have positively impacted your life recently. Who are they, and what specific actions or qualities make you grateful for their presence in your life?

Personal Achievements and Growth: Think about your recent accomplishments, no matter how big or small. What achievements are you proud of? Additionally, consider areas where you've experienced personal growth, such as overcoming a fear, or changing a habit.

Simple Pleasures: Focus on the small, everyday things that bring you joy and contentment. This could be as simple as a delicious meal, the feeling of the sun on your skin, a good book, a quiet moment for yourself, or the beauty you notice in your surroundings.

Here are 10 prompts for gratitude journaling:
1. I am grateful for this moment of calm today because...
2. Today, I appreciated myself for...
3. I felt joy when...
4. A challenge I'm thankful for is... because it taught me...
5. I am thankful for the person in my life who... because they...
6. One thing in nature that filled me with awe today was...
7. A simple pleasure that made today special is...
8. I'm grateful for my health because...
9. I felt proud of myself when...
10. The kindness I received/gave today was... it made me feel...

TRACKER

WEEK OF: _____

MY GOALS	MY FEELINGS	DONE
MON		
TUES		
WED		
THURS		
FRI		
SAT		
SUN		

Week 34: Squats while you Brush

Why: *Get a nice butt, improve leg strength, endurance, and tone your lower body.*

Who doesn't want a nice butt and more alertness in the mornings? Incorporating squats into your tooth brushing routine is an efficient multitasking habit that strengthens and tones the lower body muscles, enhances balance and coordination plus releases endorphins that boost mood and reduce stress. It offers the added benefit of promoting blood circulation, leading to increased energy and alertness, especially beneficial if done in the morning.

Weekly Goal: Do 20-50 squats in the mornings while brushing your teeth.

Stacking Strategy: Squat while you brush your teeth, think about things you are grateful for or think about plans for the day.

Tips: Motivation is deeply personal, and different strategies work for different people. It's important to find what resonates with you. Motivation can often be elusive, but here are a few strategies, hopefully one works for you:

1. Make it part of a Routine: Establish a consistent routine. Habitual behavior can foster a sense of normalcy and reduce the need for constant motivation.

2. Use Positive Reinforcement: Reward yourself for achieving milestones. This positive reinforcement can boost your motivation to continue pursuing your goals.

3. Visualize Success: Spend time visualizing achieving your goals. This mental practice can be a powerful motivator.

4. Track Your Progress: Keep track of your progress. Seeing how far you've come can be a great motivator to keep going.

TRACKER

WEEK OF: _____

MY GOALS	MY FEELINGS	DONE
MON		
TUES		
WED		
THURS		
FRI		
SAT		
SUN		

NOTES _____
_____
_____
_____
_____
_____
_____
_____
_____

Week 35: Reconnect with Someone You Lost Touch With

Why: Fostering relationships can boost mental health by providing a source of joy, reducing feelings of loneliness, and increasing feelings of self-worth and confidence for yourself and others.

Reconnecting provides an opportunity to rekindle valuable friendships, potentially leading to renewed relationships that add depth to your social life. Such reunions can also offer closure and emotional healing, especially if past issues were left unresolved. Professionally, they can open up new networking opportunities, given each person's experiences and connections formed over time. On a personal level, reminiscing shared memories can bring joy and nostalgia, while observing each other's growth can offer fresh perspectives and insights into your own life journey.

Weekly Goal: Reach out to at least one person you've lost touch with. This could be an old friend, a former colleague, or even a distant family member. The goal is to initiate contact, perhaps through a message, a phone call, or a handwritten letter.

Stacking Strategy: Integrate this task with your existing new habits such as letter writing or when practicing kindness. Alternatively, if Sunday afternoons are your downtime, include reaching out as part of your relaxing weekend routine.

Tips: The goal isn't to pick up exactly where you left off but to explore the possibility of a renewed connection in the present context.

NOTE: This week's tracker is in Week 36

To successfully reconnect with someone you've lost touch with, consider these three practical tips:

1. Reach Out in a Comfortable Medium: Start by reaching out through a medium that feels comfortable like a friendly email, a social media message, or even a phone call, depending on your previous mode of communication. Keep the message light and open-ended, expressing a genuine interest in catching up and learning about what they've been up to. Here are some sample prompts to help you get started:

    - Casual and Friendly: "Hey [Name], it's been a while! I was just thinking about our [shared experience or memory] and couldn't help but smile. How have you been? Would love to catch up and hear all about what you've been up to!"

    - Interest and Open-Ended: "Hi [Name], I hope this message finds you well. I realized it's been quite some time since we last spoke, and I'm curious to hear about your journey since then. If you're up for it, I'd really enjoy catching up. Let me know what you think!"

    - Specific and Personalized: "Hello [Name], I came across [a book, song, movie, etc.] that reminded me of our conversations about [specific topic]. It made me think about you and wonder how you're doing. Would you be interested in grabbing a coffee sometime and reconnecting?"

2. Set Realistic Expectations: Approach the reconnection without heavy expectations. People change over time, and so do their life circumstances. Go into the conversation with an open mind and a willingness to accept them as they are now, rather than how you remember them.

3. Plan an Informal Meet-up: If the initial contact goes well, suggest an informal meet-up, like grabbing a coffee or a casual lunch.

Week 36: Make your bed

Why: *Sets a positive tone for the day with an early sense of accomplishment and encourages overall organization and tidiness.*

According to Charles Duhigg, author of "The Power of Habit," making your bed is a "keystone habit" that can spark chain reactions leading to other good habits. It's believed to increase your overall productivity and organizational skills. The act of organizing your space, starting with your bed, can provide a sense of control and order in your life, potentially improving your mood and reducing anxiety. It also enhances the bedroom environment, making it a more calming space, which contributes to better sleep.

Weekly Goal: Make your bed each morning.

Stacking Strategy: Get in the habit of making your bed right after your bathroom routine. While doing the task, you can think about your daily goals, or repeat a daily mantra to start the day right.

Tips: Consider timing yourself to realize the minimal effort involved in making your bed. Simplify your bedding as much as possible by using fewer pillows and a manageable comforter or duvet that's easy to straighten and tuck in. The less complicated it is, the more likely you are to do it each morning. It's important to be patient and consistent; if you miss a day, just resume the habit the next. Over time, this simple task can lead to a more organized lifestyle and a sense of accomplishment to start your day.

TRACKER WEEK OF: _____

MY GOALS	MY FEELINGS	DONE
MON		
TUES		

MY GOALS	MY FEELINGS	DONE
WED		
THURS		
FRI		
SAT		
SUN		

WEEK OF: _____

MY GOALS	MY FEELINGS	DONE
MON		
TUES		
WED		
THURS		
FRI		
SAT		
SUN		

Week 37: Listen to a Podcast

Why: *Provides education, entertainment, and a sense of connection.*

Podcasts provide exposure to diverse perspectives and ideas, which can enhance motivation, learning, critical thinking and empathy. Additionally, they can be a source of inspiration and entertainment, making them a versatile tool for both personal and professional growth. Incorporating podcast listening into your daily routine can enrich your knowledge, broaden your horizons, and provide a meaningful use of your time.

Weekly Goal: Listen to an educational or motivational podcast.

Stacking Strategy: You can listen while out for a walk, cooking, or while doing your weekly tidy or decluttering.

Tips: Here are some popular podcasts in three categories you can try:

1. Personal Growth:
    a. Happier with Gretchen Rubin: Focuses on tactics for leading happier lives and forming beneficial habits.
    b. The Happiness Lab: Hosted by Yale professor Dr. Laurie Santos, based on the science of happiness and her popular psychology course.
    c. Optimal Living Daily: Presents top online content on self-improvement, covering topics like minimalism, personal development, and productivity.
2. Finance
    a. ChooseFI / Financial Independence Podcast: Best for those seeking financial independence through various strategies.
    b. Millennial Investing: Offers insights for millennials navigating the financial world, featuring industry leaders.
    c. Ditch the Suits: Focuses on unfiltered discussions about the financial industry and multi-generational planning.

3. Relationships:

    a. Why Won't You Date Me? with Nicole Byer: Combines humor and honesty to explore the quirks of love.

    b. Doing Relationships Right: Provides guidance for overcoming past relationships and finding the perfect match.

    c. Sextras: Offers unfiltered relationship advice for millennials, covering a wide range of topics related to love and lust.

TRACKER

WEEK OF: _____

MY GOALS	MY FEELINGS	DONE
MON		
TUES		
WED		
THURS		
FRI		
SAT		
SUN		

Week 38: No Complaints Day

***Why:** Promotes positivity, improves mood, and enhances problem-solving skills.*

Regular complaining can cement a negative outlook, impacting not only personal happiness but also relationships with others. By focusing on solutions rather than problems, you can enhance problem-solving skills and productivity. Reducing complaints leads to a more optimistic perspective, which is linked to improved mental health, reduced stress, and better coping strategies in challenging situations. Moreover, a less complaint-driven approach can improve interpersonal relationships and create a more positive environment both at home and in the workplace. Adopting this habit encourages a shift towards gratitude and constructive thinking, contributing to a healthier, more contented life.

Weekly Goal: Go one day without complaining. Try to pick one day each week for this habit, probably a Monday.

Stacking Strategy: Use your morning positive affirmation or gratitude practice to set a no-complaint tone.

Successfully adopting the habit of not complaining can be challenging, but these three tips can help you make this positive change:

Tips: Be patient with yourself and recognize that it's a gradual process. Over time, these practices can significantly reduce your inclination to complain, leading to a more positive and constructive outlook on life.

1. Practice Mindfulness and Self-Awareness: Start by becoming more aware of your thoughts and speech patterns. Mindfulness practices like meditation can help you recognize when you're about to complain. When you catch yourself complaining, pause and reflect on why you feel the need to express negativity. This awareness is the first step towards change.

2. Shift to Solution-Oriented Thinking: Instead of dwelling on the problem, train your mind to look for solutions or alternatives. When faced with a situation that prompts a complaint, ask yourself, "What

can I do about this?" or "How can I view this differently?" Focusing on solutions rather than problems can dramatically shift your mindset.

3. Cultivate Gratitude: Develop a habit of recognizing and appreciating the positive aspects of your life. Keeping a gratitude journal or simply taking a moment each day to reflect on what you're thankful for can help counterbalance the tendency to complain. Gratitude not only reduces the urge to focus on the negative but also improves overall mental well-being.

TRACKER

WEEK OF: _____

MY GOALS	MY FEELINGS	DONE
MON		
TUES		
WED		
THURS		
FRI		
SAT		
SUN		

Week 39: Explore a New Place

Why: Stimulates the mind, creates new experiences, and breaks routine.

Exploring new places is highly beneficial as it expands your worldview, stimulates creativity, and enhances adaptability. It breaks the monotony of daily life, offering a sense of adventure and mental rejuvenation. This habit also sharpens problem-solving skills and fosters personal growth, leading to a more fulfilled and enriched life experience.

Weekly Goal: Visit a new place, be it a restaurant, shop, neighborhood etc in your city or town. This could be a weekly or monthly habit.

Stacking Strategy: Combine this exploration with another regular activity or outing.

Tips: There are so many opportunities to explore new places close to home. If you do weekly grocery shopping, try visiting a market in a different area. If you enjoy weekend walks, choose a new neighborhood or park to explore each time. Or, if Friday nights are typically dine-out nights, select a new restaurant to try. By linking the exploration of new places with established routines, you're more likely to follow through and enjoy these fresh experiences regularly.

TRACKER

WEEK OF: _____

MY GOALS	MY FEELINGS	DONE
MON		
TUES		
WED		
THURS		
FRI		
SAT		
SUN		

NOTES_____
_____
_____
_____
_____
_____
_____
_____
_____
_____
_____

Week 40: Focus on Your Work

Why: Gives a sense of accomplishment and progress

Concentrating on work and being productive not only helps in achieving professional goals but also brings a sense of accomplishment, progress and attention to detail. Focusing on work can lead to better job performance, increased job satisfaction, and the development of a strong work ethic. This focus not only leads to professional growth and advancement but also contributes to reduced stress levels, as managing tasks effectively helps avoid last-minute rushes and associated anxiety.

Weekly Goal: Put your head down, and just work for 3 solid hours, ignore your phone, the noise and distractions. Schedule it in for at least one day each week.

Stacking Strategy: Right after your morning stretch, coffee or tea, spend a few minutes planning your workday.

Tips: Schedule it in, turn off your phone and outline your top priorities and goals for what you wish to accomplish. Here are 3 strategies to help you succeed:

1. Create a Distraction-Free Environment: Minimize interruptions and distractions in your workspace. This can involve turning off non-essential notifications on your phone and computer, using noise-canceling headphones, or setting up a dedicated, clutter-free area specifically for work. A clean and organized workspace can significantly enhance your ability to focus.

2. Prioritize and Plan Your Tasks: Start each day or week by prioritizing your tasks. Use techniques like the Eisenhower Box to categorize tasks by their urgency and importance. Create a realistic to-do list and allocate specific time blocks for each task.

3. Implement the Pomodoro Technique: This time management method involves working in focused intervals (traditionally 25 minutes) followed by short breaks. These intervals, known as 'Pomodoros', are effective in maintaining high levels of concentration and preventing burnout. During each Pomodoro, commit to working on just one task without any distractions. After each interval, take a 5-minute break to rest and recharge.

TRACKER

WEEK OF: _____

MY GOALS	MY FEELINGS	DONE
MON		
TUES		
WED		
THURS		
FRI		
SAT		
SUN		

NOTES_____
_____
_____
_____
_____
_____
_____
___

Week 41: Learn to Say No

Why: *Sets healthy boundaries, increases self-respect, and reduces stress, regret and resentment.*

Saying no is crucial for maintaining personal boundaries, managing stress, and ensuring a healthy work-life balance. Research in the field of psychology underscores that not being able to say no can lead to increased stress and anxiety, as well as a decrease in work-life balance. This can negatively impact mental health and overall life satisfaction. Furthermore, studies on workplace productivity show that overcommitment, often due to an inability to say no, can lead to decreased productivity and job satisfaction. By saying no, individuals are better able to prioritize tasks and commitments that align with their personal and professional goals, leading to a more balanced and fulfilling life.

Weekly Goal: Focus on politely declining requests or invitations that do not align with your priorities or values. The goal is to assert your decision firmly but kindly, ensuring that you are respecting both your own boundaries and the other person's feelings.

Stacking Strategy: Whenever faced with a request or an opportunity, take a moment to practice mindful breathing and evaluate it against your priorities. Pair this with your regular reflection or journaling routine to assess situations where you might need to say 'no' and plan your approach.

Tips: Here are some examples of how to say 'no':
- "Thank you for thinking of me, but I won't be able to participate this time."
- "I appreciate the offer, but I'm currently focusing on other priorities and won't have the time to commit to this."
- "I can't join you for dinner this Friday, but how about we meet for lunch next week instead?"
- "I wish I could, but..." or "I'd love to, but unfortunately..."
- "I need to say no for now, but I really appreciate your offer."

In all cases, keeping your response clear, concise, and respectful is key. It's also important to remember that it's okay to prioritize your own needs and that saying no is a part of healthy communication.

TRACKER

WEEK OF: _____

MY GOALS	MY FEELINGS	DONE
MON		
TUES		
WED		
THURS		
FRI		
SAT		
SUN		

NOTES _____

Week 42: Learn to Say Yes

Why: *Open doors to new opportunities, experiences, and connections plus personal development, new friendships, and unexpected adventures.*

Saying yes opens up opportunities for new experiences, personal growth, and learning, which are key components for a fulfilling life. Studies in positive psychology suggest that saying yes to new challenges can increase adaptability and resilience, and contribute to a growth mindset. This approach encourages individuals to step out of their comfort zones, leading to enhanced self-esteem and confidence. However, it's important to balance the willingness to say yes with the understanding of one's limits to avoid overcommitment (i.e. saying no).

Weekly Goal: Weekly, make a conscious effort to accept an invitation or opportunity that you might typically decline due to hesitation or fear.

Stacking Strategy: Align this practice with your daily or weekly planning, doing something uncomfortable practice and during self-reflection. Use mindful breathing before making a decision.

Tips: Focus on saying 'yes' to things that align with your values and interests, even if they challenge you or push your boundaries.

When to say Yes: When reviewing your schedule or considering new opportunities, actively look for instances where you can say 'yes.' This could be as simple as agreeing to a social event, taking on a new project, or trying a new hobby. Combine this with moments of self-reflection to understand why you might usually say 'no' and how saying 'yes' could benefit you. This approach helps you become more intentional about embracing new experiences and stepping into growth opportunities.

TRACKER

WEEK OF: _____

MY GOALS	MY FEELINGS	DONE
MON		
TUES		
WED		
THURS		
FRI		
SAT		
SUN		

NOTES _____
_____
_____
_____
_____
_____
_____
_____
_____
_____
_____

Week 43: Correct Something you Are Doing Wrong

Why: *Crucial for self-improvement and growth. Helps personal development, enhances relationships and professional life and fosters responsibility and integrity.*

Acknowledging and addressing mistakes or inefficiencies allows for learning and improvement, fostering a growth mindset. This practice not only enhances skills and knowledge but also builds resilience and adaptability, key traits for success and satisfaction in various life aspects. Moreover, taking responsibility for errors and actively working to correct them strengthens integrity and trustworthiness in both personal and professional relationships.

Weekly Goal: Each week or day identify a specific behavior, habit, or mistake that you realize is not serving you well. This could range from a small daily habit to a more significant behavioral pattern. Ask yourself what you can do to fix it. Commit to making a conscious effort to correct or improve this aspect throughout the week.

Stacking Strategy: Tie this goal with your daily planning or journaling routine. During this time, reflect on the behavior you want to correct, and plan actionable steps to address it.

Tips: Correcting your mistakes isn't to be overly critical of yourself, but to foster growth and improvement. Be patient and persistent, as change often takes time.To effectively correct something you are doing wrong, consider these three tips:

1. Embrace Self-Reflection: Regularly take time for self-reflection to assess your actions and decisions. Identify areas where you might be falling short or making mistakes. Honest self-assessment is the first step in recognizing and addressing what you need to change.

2. Seek Feedback and Constructive Criticism: Don't hesitate to ask for feedback from others, whether it's colleagues, friends, or family. Others can offer valuable perspectives on areas you might overlook. Be open to constructive criticism and use it as a tool for improvement.

3. Create an Action Plan: Once you've identified what needs to be corrected, develop a clear action plan. This should include specific steps to change the behavior or process, along with measurable goals and timelines. Regularly review your progress and be willing to adjust your plan as needed.

TRACKER

WEEK OF: _____

MY GOALS	MY FEELINGS	DONE
MON		
TUES		
WED		
THURS		
FRI		
SAT		
SUN		

NOTES_____
_____
_____
_____

Week 44: Daily Laughter

Why: *Reduces stress, enhances mood, and can even improve immunity.*

Laugh for health! Laughter triggers the release of endorphins, the body's natural feel-good chemicals, promoting an overall sense of well-being (Journal of Neuroscience). Laughter can reduce stress by lowering cortisol levels (American Journal of the Medical Sciences) and physiologically, it improves cardiac health by enhancing blood flow and vascular function, according to research in the "American Journal of Cardiology." Additionally, laughter has been found to boost the immune system, improve pain tolerance, and enhance social bonding and communication, as detailed in studies in "Psychosomatic Medicine" and other psychological journals. Overall, laughter acts as a powerful tool for stress relief, pain reduction, and strengthening social connections, making it an important aspect of both mental and physical health.

Weekly Goal: Make it your goal to find a reason to laugh heartily every day.

Stacking Strategy: Integrate laughter into your existing daily routines with a funny show or podcast while decluttering or cooking. Alternatively read a humorous book before bed.

Tips: Relax and not take yourself too seriously. Laughter should be a fun and enjoyable part of life. Here's ways to incorporate more laughter into your life:
1. Seek Out Humor: Can be watching a funny video, sharing a joke with a friend, or recalling a humorous memory.
2. Spend Time with Funny People: Interact with friends or family members who have a good sense of humor. People who laugh easily and often can encourage you to do the same.
3. Fake It Till You Make It: Even forced laughter can lead to genuine laughter. Start with a fake laugh and let it evolve.
4. Play and Be Silly: Dance, be goofy and playful can naturally lead to laughter.
5. Use Technology: Social media, or websites dedicated to humor.
6. Smile More: Smiling can be a precursor to laughter.

TRACKER

WEEK OF: _____

MY GOALS	MY FEELINGS	DONE
MON		
TUES		
WED		
THURS		
FRI		
SAT		
SUN		

NOTES _____

Week 45: Avoid Processed Food

Why Improves overall health, supports weight management, and enhances energy levels.

The high calorie, low nutrient profile of processed foods, coupled with their addictive qualities, as suggested by research in "Public Health Nutrition," can lead to overeating and weight gain. Research consistently indicates that a diet high in processed foods can have detrimental health effects. Processed foods often contain high levels of added sugars, sodium, and unhealthy fats, which are linked to an increased risk of chronic diseases such as obesity, heart disease, and type 2 diabetes, as shown in studies published in journals like "BMJ" and "The American Journal of Clinical Nutrition." These foods are typically low in essential nutrients and fiber, leading to poor nutritional quality and digestive issues. Additionally, research in the "British Medical Journal" has associated processed food consumption with higher rates of depression and reduced psychological well-being.

Weekly Goal: Cut processed foods by at least half and instead eat whole, natural foods.

Stacking Strategy: Pair this habit with your cooking routine, exploring new recipes that use fresh, unprocessed ingredients.

Tips: Focusing on whole foods, such as fruits, vegetables, lean proteins, and whole grains, while avoiding or limiting highly processed foods, can significantly improve overall health. Here are 5 ingredients you should try to avoid:

1. Trans Fats: Often listed as "partially hydrogenated oils" on ingredient labels, trans fats are associated with an increased risk of heart disease. They raise bad cholesterol (LDL) and lower good cholesterol (HDL).

2. High Fructose Corn Syrup (HFCS): A common sweetener in many processed foods and beverages, HFCS has been linked to obesity, type 2 diabetes, and heart disease. It can contribute to increased belly fat and insulin resistance.

3. Artificial Sweeteners: While used as a sugar substitute, aspartame, sucralose, and saccharin may have negative effects on metabolism, gut bacteria, and appetite regulation. Their long-term health impacts are still being studied.

4. Sodium Nitrate/Nitrite: Used as preservatives in processed meats, these compounds can form nitrosamines in the body, which are potentially carcinogenic. High intake is linked to an increased risk of cancers, particularly colorectal cancer.

5. Artificial Colors and Dyes: Artificial colors like Red 40, Yellow 5, and Blue 1 have been linked to behavioral issues in children, including hyperactivity and attention deficits, and potential carcinogenic effects.

TRACKER

WEEK OF: _____

MY GOALS	MY FEELINGS	DONE
MON		
TUES		
WED		
THURS		
FRI		
SAT		
SUN		

Week 46: Learn a New Word

Why: gain a richer vocabulary to better communicate and impress!

Learning a new word on a regular basis is an excellent way to enhance your vocabulary, which directly improves communication skills. A richer vocabulary allows for more precise and expressive communication, which is beneficial both personally and professionally. It also stimulates cognitive function, as learning new words challenges your brain, keeping it active and engaged. This practice can also boost confidence in writing and speaking, and it fosters a deeper understanding and appreciation of the language.

Stacking Strategy: Use in your journaling, letter writing or meditation.

Weekly Goal: Incorporate at least one new word into your vocabulary each week.

Tips: Use this word in different contexts to ensure you understand and remember it. Here

1. Incorporate Technology: Tools like "Word of the Day" app, provide a new word daily along with its meaning, usage, and sometimes even its etymology, making it easy and convenient to learn on the go.

2. Contextual Learning: Whenever you learn a new word, try to use it in various sentences throughout the day in conversations or emails. This contextual usage helps in cementing the word in your memory.

3. Keep a Vocabulary Journal: Every day, add the new word, its definition, a sentence using it, and any synonyms or antonyms. Regularly reviewing this journal can reinforce your learning and track your progress.

TRACKER

WEEK OF: _____

MY GOALS	MY FEELINGS	DONE
MON		
TUES		
WED		
THURS		
FRI		
SAT		
SUN		

NOTES _____

Week 47: Early Dinner

Why: *Aids digestion, improves sleep quality, and helps in weight management.*

Research supports the health benefits of eating an early dinner, linking it to improved digestion, better sleep quality, and potential weight loss. It aligns with the body's circadian rhythm, aiding digestion and metabolism and reduces the risk of gastrointestinal discomfort. This can contribute to better sleep, as the body isn't working hard on digestion during rest.

Weekly Goal: Finish dinner at least 3 hours before bedtime.

Stacking Strategy: Combine with fasting and nighttime routine.

Tips: To establish the habit of eating an early dinner:

1. Plan Your Meals: Organize and prepare your meals in advance. Planning helps in aligning dinner time with your schedule, ensuring you eat earlier.

2. Set a Fixed Dinner Time: Determine a specific time for dinner. This consistency helps your body adapt to a new routine.

3. Eat Light at Night: Choose lighter, easily digestible meals for dinner. Heavier meals take longer to digest, tempting you to eat later.

Here are two meal ideas that are nutritious, flavorful, and can be prepared in under 15 minutes:

- Lemon Garlic Chicken: Sauté chicken breast strips in olive oil with garlic, lemon juice, salt, and pepper until cooked through. Serve with a side of rice, steamed vegetables or a simple salad.

- Chickpea Stir-fry: Sauté canned chickpeas with bell peppers, onions, garlic, and your choice of quick-cooking vegetables like spinach or zucchini. Season with soy sauce, ginger, and a hint of sesame oil. Serve this over pre-cooked rice or quinoa for a wholesome meal.

TRACKER

WEEK OF: _____

MY GOALS	MY FEELINGS	DONE
MON		
TUES		
WED		
THURS		
FRI		
SAT		
SUN		

NOTES _____
_____
_____
_____
_____
_____
_____
_____
_____

Week 48: Practice Patience

Why: Reduces stress, improves decision-making, and enhances relationships.

Practicing patience is crucial for mental well-being, relationship building, and personal and professional success. It helps in managing stress and reducing the impulsivity that can lead to rash decisions and conflicts. Patience allows for a more thoughtful, empathetic approach to interactions with others, improving communication and understanding. It's also linked to better mental health, with research suggesting that patient individuals often experience lower levels of depression and higher overall life satisfaction.

Weekly Goal: Aim to identify and reflect on at least three specific instances where practicing patience made a positive difference in your day or interactions.

Stacking Strategy: Use conscious breathing for an added breath towards patience, and journal challenges and experiences, triggers and outcomes.

Tips: To effectively practice patience, consider these three practical tips:

1. Mindfulness and Deep Breathing: When you feel impatience creeping up, pause and engage in deep breathing. This helps to calm your mind and body, allowing you to approach situations with a more patient and clear perspective.

2. Reflect on the Benefits of Patience: Regularly remind yourself of the positive outcomes patience can bring, such as better decision-making, improved relationships, and reduced stress.

3. Pause Before Reacting: In moments of potential frustration or impatience, take a brief pause before responding. This short break can give you time to gather your thoughts and respond in a more measured, patient manner, rather than reacting impulsively.

TRACKER

WEEK OF: _____

MY GOALS	MY FEELINGS	DONE
MON		
TUES		
WED		
THURS		
FRI		
SAT		
SUN		

NOTES _____
_____
_____
_____
_____
_____
_____
_____
_____

Week 49: Practice Forgiveness

Why: *Reduces stress, improves mental health, and fosters healthier relationships.*

Anger and resentment does not serve you and it may actually be harming you. Instead learn to create boundaries and understanding. Research has consistently shown that forgiveness is linked to lower levels of stress, anxiety, and depression. A study published in the "Journal of Health Psychology" found that forgiveness is associated with better mental health outcomes and lower psychological distress. Moreover, forgiving others can lead to improvements in physical health, with reduced blood pressure and a lower risk of heart disease, as indicated in research from the "American Journal of Cardiology." Overall, practicing forgiveness as a habit can lead to a more peaceful, healthier, and fulfilling life, both mentally and physically.

Weekly Goal: Forgive someone or let go of a past grudge. This could be a minor incident or a more significant grievance. The aim is to consciously release any negative feelings tied to this person or event.

Stacking Strategy: Incorporate into reaching out to someone, writing a letter, your daily reflection or meditation routine.

Tips: This habit is extremely challenging for many due to the pain, trauma or shame that may be associated. You may not feel like forgiving and perhaps it feels like staying angry somehow protects you. But I encourage you to believe that forgiveness will benefit you more than you realize. As quoted by Will Smith, " There is so much joy on the other side of fear".

Forgiveness is a process and might not happen overnight. Be patient with yourself as you work through your feelings and thoughts. Here is how you can get started:

1. Reflect and Acknowledge: During a quiet time acknowledging your feelings about the situation and the impact it has had on you. Reflect on the incident objectively, understanding that holding onto resentment often causes more harm to yourself than to the other person.

2. Empathy and Understanding: Try to see the situation from the other person's perspective. This doesn't mean excusing their behavior, but understanding their motives or circumstances can sometimes make it easier to forgive. Empathy is a key component in the process of forgiveness.

3. Actively Choose to Forgive: Forgiveness is an active choice, not just a feeling. Make a conscious decision to forgive, even if it feels difficult. You can do this through a verbal affirmation, writing it down, or even directly communicating with the person involved if appropriate. Remember, forgiveness is more for your peace of mind and well-being than for the other person.

4. If Needed, Create Boundaries: Creating boundaries is essential for maintaining personal well-being and healthy relationships. A key tip for establishing boundaries is to communicate them clearly and assertively. Start by identifying your limits in various aspects of life, such as time, energy, and emotional capacity.

5. Wherever Legal, Psychedelics as a Therapeutic Tool: Research indicates that psychedelics like psilocybin and MDMA may aid in emotional healing and forgiveness. Studies, including those from Johns Hopkins University and published in the "Journal of Psychopharmacology," show that these substances can enhance well-being, empathy, and openness, especially in clinical settings like treating life-threatening illnesses or PTSD. They work by reducing ego defenses and ingrained thought patterns, allowing a new perspective on emotions and experiences. However, this research is still developing, and the use of psychedelics is usually in controlled environments with professional guidance, highlighting the importance of context in their therapeutic effectiveness

TRACKER

WEEK OF: _____

MY GOALS	MY FEELINGS	DONE
MON		
TUES		
WED		
THURS		
FRI		
SAT		
SUN		

Week 50: Allow Something to Take your Breath Away

Why: *"The most beautiful thing we can experience is the mysterious. It is the source of all true art and science." Albert Einstein*

Experiencing moments that take your breath away is vital for maintaining a sense of wonder and appreciation for life. These awe-inspiring moments can provide a much-needed pause from the routine, offering fresh perspectives and heightened emotional states. Research suggests that experiencing awe can enhance mood, boost creativity, and even improve physical health by reducing stress.

Weekly Goal: Actively seek and appreciate awe-inspiring moments in daily life, every day, at least once to jot in your journal or mind.

Stacking Strategy: Combine during walks, evening nighttime routine, or while reading about awe-inspiring topics.

Tips: There is wonder all around, but if you need a little inspiration here are some ideas for you. Remember to take a moment to reflect on how it made you feel and the thoughts it provoked.

1. Explore Nature: Spend time in natural settings that are known for their beauty and grandeur. This could be as simple as watching a sunset, stargazing, or visiting a nearby park or natural reserve.

2. Seek Out Art and Culture: Engage with art forms that move you. Visit art galleries, attend live performances, or listen to music that stirs deep emotions.

3. Learn About the Universe: The vastness and mystery of the universe can be incredibly awe-inspiring. Spend time learning about space, watching documentaries, or reading books on astronomy and cosmology.

TRACKER

WEEK OF: _____

MY GOALS	MY FEELINGS	DONE
MON		
TUES		
WED		
THURS		
FRI		
SAT		
SUN		

Week 51: Reflect on Achievements

Why: *Boosts self-esteem, provides motivation, and acknowledges personal growth.*

Significant change often starts with small manageable steps. It is the accumulation of your small wins that result in long term transformation. Reflecting on achievements these past 50 weeks is crucial for personal growth and motivation. It provides a sense of accomplishment and reinforces positive self-esteem and confidence. This practice helps in acknowledging progress, no matter how small, which is essential for maintaining motivation and persistence towards long-term goals. It also offers valuable insights into what strategies work, allowing for more effective future planning. Psychologically, celebrating achievements, even minor ones, activates the brain's reward pathways, contributing to a positive mindset and greater job satisfaction. Moreover, this reflection fosters gratitude and a positive outlook, crucial elements for overall well-being and resilience in the face of challenges.

Weekly Goal: This week use the worksheets in the Appendix to reflect on your achievements. If you've made it this far, even if no habit has stuck with you, you still stayed committed to the process and that is huge!

Stacking Strategy: Review your Weekly Trackers, journals and reflections and enjoy reflection, conscious breathing and being in the moment as you reflect..

Tips: Small steps, often overlooked in the pursuit of larger goals, play a crucial role in achieving significant progress and success. These incremental actions lay the foundation for substantial change, yet their subtlety frequently leads to them being undervalued or unnoticed in our reflections and assessments. It's a reminder that consistent, small efforts lead to transformative results that might not be immediately visible.

Reflecting on these small steps is vital as it helps us recognize and value our progress, reinforcing the belief in our ability. This practice of acknowledging even the minutest of achievements is not only motivational but also builds a narrative of perseverance and growth! It teaches us the power of persistence and patience, highlighting that impactful results often stem from modest but consistent efforts. Here are some reflections for you to review:

1. **Overall Reflection**
   - Successes: List the major successes of the year.
   - Challenges: Reflect on any challenges faced and how they were overcome.
   - Growth & Development: Analyze areas of personal growth and development.
   - Lessons Learned: Note any key lessons learned throughout the year.

2. **Feedback and Inputs**
   - Feedback from Others: Summarize feedback received from friends.
   - Self-Assessment: Write a self-assessment of your journey.

TRACKER

WEEK OF: _____

MY GOALS	MY FEELINGS	DONE
MON		
TUES		
WED		
THURS		
FRI		
SAT		
SUN		

Week 52: Plan for the Next Year

You've spent the last 51 weeks exploring and integrating various habits into your life, gaining insights into what works and doesn't work, what motivates you and how to habit stack. Armed with this knowledge, this week, we encourage you to take a step further by creating your own habit. This is an opportunity to tailor a habit(s) specifically to your personal goals, interests, and lifestyle.

Objective:

- Develop a personalized habit that aligns with your individual needs and aspirations.
- Utilize the skills and insights you've gained throughout this journey to create a habit that will contribute significantly to your personal growth, health and/or fulfillment.

Instructions:

1. Reflect on Your Journey: Think back on the past 50 weeks. Which habits resonated most with you? What areas of your life have you most enjoyed improving?

2. Identify Your Needs and Goals: What areas of your life do you feel could still use improvement or attention? What personal goals do you have that you haven't yet addressed?

3. Brainstorm Habit Ideas: Based on your reflections, brainstorm potential habits that align with your goals. Think creatively and don't limit yourself..

4. Define the Habit: Once you have an idea, define it clearly. What exactly will you do? How often? When and where will you do it? And please share it with our community.

5. Plan for Implementation: Consider any tools, resources, or changes in routine you might need to successfully implement this habit. How will you integrate it into your existing routine?

6. Use a Tracking Method: Decide how you will track your progress. Will you use a journal, an app, or a checklist?

7. Commit to a Time Frame: Just like the other habits, commit to trying this new habit for a set period. You might choose one week, one month, or longer.

Examples:

- If fitness has been your favorite area, your habit could be a specific type of exercise, like yoga three times a week.
- If you've enjoyed habits around mindfulness, you might create a habit of daily evening reflection or gratitude.

Reflection: At the end of your chosen time frame, reflect on this habit. Did it benefit you? Do you want to continue, modify, or replace it?

Encouragement: Remember, the key to this habit is personalization. This is your journey, and you have the freedom to design a habit that truly enriches your life and brings you closer to your ultimate goals.

TRACKER

WEEK OF: _____

MY GOALS	MY FEELINGS	DONE
MON		
TUES		
WED		
THURS		
FRI		
SAT		
SUN		

4. You are Fabulous

Congratulations on giving "52 Weekly Habits" a try! Over the past year, you've explored a variety of habits, each designed to enhance different aspects of your life, from health and productivity to mindfulness and personal growth. The key takeaway from this journey is the power from small, consistent actions and how they can bring about significant change.

Remember, the goal was never about perfection or rigidly adhering to every habit, but about exploring what works best for you and discovering new ways to enrich your life with small habits. Because small habits add up to big transformation.

As you move forward, carry with you the habits that resonated most, create your own and feel empowered to continue adapting and evolving your routine. There is a Monday every week and a morning every day to start fresh! The journey of self-improvement is ongoing, and I hope the skills and insights you've gained over the past 52 weeks provided a strong foundation for continued growth, fulfillment and health.

Celebrate the progress you've made, no matter how big or small, and recognize the effort and dedication it took to reach this point. The habits you've cultivated are now tools in your arsenal for a happier, healthier, and more productive life. You can re-start them at any time! Here's to the changes you've made, the resilience you've built, and the journey ahead. Keep moving forward, one small habit, at a time.

> "
> Small habits add up to big transformation.
> "

5. Appendix

52 WEEKLY HABITS

Week 1: Practice Deep Breathing
Week 2: Drink More Water
Week 3: 2min Stretch
Week 4: Practice Good Posture
Week 5: Journaling
Week 6: Mindful Eating
Week 7: Daily Walking
Week 8: Improve Sleep Routine
Week 9: Decluttering
Week 10: Reduce Screen Time
Week 11: Healthy Snacking
Week 12: Oil Pulling
Week 13: Morning Meditation
Week 14: Morning Affirmations
Week 15: Morning Phone Detox
Week 16: Night Time Phone Detox
Week 17: Practice Kindness
Week 18: Read Before Bed
Week 19: Do Something Uncomfortable
Week 20: Early Morning Rise
Week 21: Sugar Free Day
Week 22: Have a Buddha Smile
Week 23: Conscious Breathing
Week 24: Morning Sun Salutation
Week 25: Take the Stairs
Week 26: Mid-Year Reflection

Week 27: Create a Vision Board
Week 28: Nighttime Routine
Week 29: Fast After Dinner
Week 30: Explore Nature
Week 31: Learn Something New
Week 32: Write a Letter
Week 33: Express Gratitude
Week 34: Squats while you Brush
Week 35: Reconnect with Someone You Lost Touch With
Week 36: Make your bed
Week 37: Listen to a Podcast
Week 38: No Complaints Day
Week 39: Explore a New Place
Week 40: Focus on Your Work
Week 41: Learn to Say 'No'
Week 42: Learn to Say 'Yes'
Week 43: Correct Something you Are Doing Wrong
Week 44: Daily Laughter
Week 45: Avoid Processed Food
Week 46: Learn a New Word
Week 47: Early Dinner
Week 48: Practice Patience
Week 49: Practice Forgiveness
Week 50: Allow Something to Take your Breath Away
Week 51: Reflect on Achievements
Week 52: Plan for the Next Year

Like someone counting down the days, we are counting down 52 weeks of daily habits. Each day check off the little circle if you completed any of the habits in this book intentionally. By the end of the year this will be a quick visual that shows how much you did. It is meant to inspire you, don't worry if you don't get all the days or even for that matter only 10% of the days.

HABIT TRACKER

52 HABITS	Simply cross out each day you did a habit intentionally

JAN	FEB	MAR	APR	MAY	JUN	JUL	AUG	SEP	OCT	NOV	DES
1	1	1	1	1	1	1	1	1	1	1	1
2	2	2	2	2	2	2	2	2	2	2	2
3	3	3	3	3	3	3	3	3	3	3	3
4	4	4	4	4	4	4	4	4	4	4	4
5	5	5	5	5	5	5	5	5	5	5	5
6	6	6	6	6	6	6	6	6	6	6	6
7	7	7	7	7	7	7	7	7	7	7	7
8	8	8	8	8	8	8	8	8	8	8	8
9	9	9	9	9	9	9	9	9	9	9	9
10	10	10	10	10	10	10	10	10	10	10	10
11	11	11	11	11	11	11	11	11	11	11	11
12	12	12	12	12	12	12	12	12	12	12	12
13	13	13	13	13	13	13	13	13	13	13	13
14	14	14	14	14	14	14	14	14	14	14	14
15	15	15	15	15	15	15	15	15	15	15	15
16	16	16	16	16	16	16	16	16	16	16	16
17	17	17	17	17	17	17	17	17	17	17	17
18	18	18	18	18	18	18	18	18	18	18	18
19	19	19	19	19	19	19	19	19	19	19	19
20	20	20	20	20	20	20	20	20	20	20	20
21	21	21	21	21	21	21	21	21	21	21	21
22	22	22	22	22	22	22	22	22	22	22	22
23	23	23	23	23	23	23	23	23	23	23	23
24	24	24	24	24	24	24	24	24	24	24	24
25	25	25	25	25	25	25	25	25	25	25	25
26	26	26	26	26	26	26	26	26	26	26	26
27	27	27	27	27	27	27	27	27	27	27	27
28	28	28	28	28	28	28	28	28	28	28	28
29	29	29	29	29	29	29	29	29	29	29	29
30	30	30	30	30	30	30	30	30	30	30	30
31	31	31	31	31	31	31	31	31	31	31	31

BRAINSTORMING

ACTION BRAINSTORMING CAN HELP IDENTIFY WHAT THINGS ARE
HELPING OR STOPPING YOU FROM ACHIEVING YOUR GOALS.

<u>MY
GOALS:</u>

STOP DOING

DO LESS OF

KEEP DOING

DO MORE OF

START DOING

ANALYSIS

A SWOT ANALYSIS IS OFTEN USED BY BUSINESSES BUT CAN ALSO BE USED TO IDENTIFY YOUR STRENGTHS, WEAKNESSES, OPPORTUNITIES AND THREATS. FILL OUT THE BOXES BELOW TO FIND OUT YOURS!

STRENGTHS

WEAKNESSES

OPPORTUNITIES

THREATS

HABIT STACKING PLAN

IDENTIFY ANCHORS

1. IDENTIFY HABITS YOU ALREADY DO CONSISTENTLY WITHOUT MUCH THOUGHT.
Morning Routine Anchor: Brushing teeth
Midday Routine Anchor: Lunch break
Evening Routine Anchor: Watching TV after dinner

SELECT NEW HABIT

2. CHOOSE NEW HABITS THAT YOU WANT TO DEVELOP. THESE SHOULD BE SIMPLE ENOUGH TO ADD TO YOUR ANCHOR HABITS WITHOUT FEELING OVERWHELMING.
Morning New Habit: 5 minutes of meditation
Midday New Habit: 10 minutes of reading a book
Evening New Habit: 15 minutes of stretching or yoga.

CREATE HABIT STACK

3. COMBINE YOUR NEW HABITS WITH THE ANCHOR HABITS. WRITE DOWN THE SEQUENCES.
Morning Stack: Wake up → Brush teeth → Meditate for 5 minutes.
Midday Stack: Start lunch break → Read a book for 10 minutes → Have lunch.
Evening Stack: Finish dinner → Watch TV → 15 minutes of stretching or yoga.

IDENTIFY ANCHORS

4. BEGIN IMPLEMENTING YOUR HABIT STACKS. KEEP A DAILY LOG TO TRACK YOUR CONSISTENCY AND PROGRESS.
- Start small with habits that require minimal effort.
- Perform your habit stacks at the same time each day to establish a routine.
- If a stack isn't working, don't be afraid to modify it.
- Acknowledge your achievements, no matter how small.

52WEEKLYHABITS.COM

Originally from Chile where family and a relaxed lifestyle are cherished, Paula grew up in North Vancouver surrounded by ambitious and charismatic people. She's a lively mother of three, mixing her vibrant Chilean roots with a practical, goal-driven approach. Her favorite saying, "better than nothing," started as a family joke but became her guiding principle: every little step counts. Paula finds her biggest inspiration in seeing her kids make small, steady progress towards big achievements, without stressing over huge goals.

> **" Small habits add up to big transformation. "**

Manufactured by Amazon.ca
Acheson, AB